HAMLET,

A TRAGEDY IN FIVE ACTS,

BY

WILLIAM SHAKESPEARE,

AS ARRANGED FOR THE STAGE

BY

HENRY IRVING,

AND PRESENTED AT

THE LYCEUM THEATRE,

ON MONDAY, DECEMBER 30TH, 1878.

LONDON:

PRINTED AT THE CHISWICK PRESS.

1883.

PRICE ONE SHILLING.

HAMLET,

A TRAGEDY IN FIVE ACTS,

BY

WILLIAM SHAKESPEARE,

AS ARRANGED FOR THE STAGE

BY

HENRY IRVING,

AND PRESENTED AT

THE LYCEUM THEATRE

ON MONDAY, DECEMBER 30TH, 1878.

REVISED EDITION.

LONDON:
PRINTED AT THE CHISWICK PRESS.
1883.

CHISWICK PRESS:—C. WHITTINGHAM AND CO., TOOKS COURT,
CHANCERY LANE.

PREFACE.

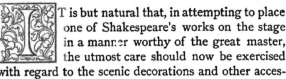

T is but natural that, in attempting to place one of Shakespeare's works on the stage in a manner worthy of the great master, the utmost care should now be exercised with regard to the scenic decorations and other accessories of the play. We live in an age remarkable for the completeness of its dramatic representations in this respect at least; and it would be showing very scant honour to the poet, whose fame is one of our dearest national possessions, were we to treat his works with less generosity and less artistic care, as regards the scenery, than the works of inferior authors. The first object of a manager, no doubt, should be to obtain capable representatives of the various characters of the play; but, having done that, their efforts will be aided and not hampered by a due attention to the effectiveness and beauty of their scenic surroundings. Shakespeare, if well acted on a bare stage, would certainly afford great intellectual pleasure; but that pleasure will be all the greater if the eye be charmed, at the same time, by scenic illustrations in harmony with the poet's ideas. Many are thus brought to listen with pleasure to the noblest works of dramatic art, who might otherwise turn away from them as dull and unattractive.

Without attempting to overburden the play with spectacular effect, and to smother the poet under a mass of decoration, it has been the object of Mr. Irving, in the present production of " Hamlet," to obtain as much picturesque effect from the assistance of the scene-painter's art as the poet's own descriptions may seem to justify. It must be remembered that, as far as the stage business and all the scenery is concerned, it is only from allusions in the text of Shakespeare's plays that we can obtain any information. He himself has given us no directions as to the scenes, and even the division into acts, in the case of " Hamlet," is not to be found in any of the editions published in his life-time. It would be easy, in such a matter, to achieve novelty at the cost of probability, and peculiarity at the cost of appropriateness. A better method is one which Shakespeare himself has commended, through the mouth of " Hamlet," with regard to dramatic poetry,

"An honest method, as wholesome as sweet, and by very much more handsome than fine."

Act ii., sc. 2, lines 429, 430.

Such a method has been aimed at in whatever innovations have been introduced into the scenery of " Hamlet" in the present representation. The principal features of such innovations may now be pointed out, as well as the reasons for their adoption.

In Act I., the first scene has been so constructed as to allow of the Ghost appearing to Marcellus, Bernardo, and Horatio on the battlements of the Castle, and not, as generally arranged, merely crossing over the front portion of the stage.[1] It must be observed that this scene is supposed to occupy the space of time between midnight and dawn. Bernardo says (line 6) :—

---

[1] A similar improvement was introduced by Mr. Tom Taylor in his arrangement of " Hamlet," produced under his superintendence at the Crystal Palace in 1873.

"'Tis now struck twelve; "

and Horatio says (lines 166, 167) :—

> " But, look, the morn, in russet mantle clad,
> Walks o'er the dew of yon high eastward hill :"

so that the painter must try and convey the impression of on-coming dawn.   In the sky may be seen the star of which Bernardo speaks (line 35) :—

" When yond same star that's westward from the pole," &c.

In the last scene of this act Hamlet is supposed to have followed the Ghost to a spot some distance from the Castle. This deviation from the usual plan has been suggested by the words of Horatio :—

> " What if it tempt you toward the flood, my lord,
> Or to the dreadful summit of the cliff
> That beetles o'er his base into the sea," &c.
> Act i., sc. 4, lines 69-71.

Also by Hamlet's exclamation,

> " I'll go no further."
> Scene v., line 1.

The old direction *Another part of the platform*, is supported by no particular reason or authority ; while the time that elapses from the first appearance of the Ghost to the time when it takes its leave of Hamlet (from midnight to dawn), as well as the fact that Marcellus and Horatio had, evidently, some difficulty in finding Hamlet, both point to the conclusion that they had come some distance from the Castle. Such a solemn revelation as the " father's spirit " has to make to his son, is made with more effect in a lonely spot than under the very walls of the Castle within which Claudius and his boon companions are feasting.

The next point that calls for any notice is in the last scene of Act III., " The Queen's Closet." This has been represented, as usual, as an ante-room to her bed chamber, hung with tapestry, and one portion of it fitted up as an oratory. The Ghost enters not in "armour," but in a kind of dressing robe (the "*night gowne*" of the stage direction in the first quarto): this is more consonant with Hamlet's exclamation :—

> "My father in his habit as he lived !"
>
> Act iii., sc. 4, line 132.

He passes through the door leading into the bed-chamber, just as he might have done in his life-time ; that chamber which has been desecrated by the faith-less Queen. This simple action of the reproachful spirit of his father may well recall to Hamlet the solemn injunction laid upon him at their first meet-ing :—

> "Let not the royal bed of Denmark be
> A couch for luxury and damnèd incest."
>
> Act i., sc. 5, lines 82, 83.

In the fifth act the representation of the Church Yard Scene has been considerably altered from that com-monly given on the stage. The church is supposed to be built on the hill above the royal palace, and the pro-cession is seen coming slowly up the ascent just as evening is changing into night. It was at this time "the maimed rites" used to be performed over the dead who

> "Did with desperate hand
> Fordo" their "own life."
>
> Act v., sc. 1, lines 208, 209.

The stars are beginning to shine faintly on the sad group gathered around the grave. Hamlet advances out of the friendly darkness which had hitherto aided his concealment, as he exclaims :—

> "What is he whose grief
> Bears such an emphasis ? whose phrase of sorrow
> Conjures the wandering stars and makes them stand
> Like wonder-wounded hearers ?"
>
> Act v., sc. 1, lines 243-246.

These words of Hamlet's might possibly have been spoken in the daylight; but they furnish a sufficient justification, in conjunction with the custom which has been alluded to above, for the innovation here introduced.[1] The second scene of this act, in which Osric appears, is supposed to take place out of doors, in the garden of the Castle. It is singular that neither Capel, Rowe, nor Theobald, when they placed this scene in " A Hall of the Palace," should have remarked on the inappropriateness of Hamlet's request to Osric to put his hat on :—

> " Put your bonnet to its right use, 'tis for the head."
>
> Act v., sc. 2, line 92.

—a request which he repeats (line 102); surely Hamlet would scarcely have addressed such words to one below him in rank, except in the open air. Indeed the whole passage seems to point to the same conclusion :—

> " *Osric.* I thank your lordship, it is very hot.
> *Hamlet.* No, believe me; 'tis very cold; the wind is northerly."

On the other hand, Hamlet says further on :—

---

[1] It will be seen that, by this arrangement, an interval of about twelve hours is supposed to elapse between Scenes 1 and 2. This is more natural than to make the action continuous; it is scarcely probable that immediately on leaving Ophelia's grave the King would propose this fencing match between Laertes and Hamlet, or that they would consent to the proposal at such a moment. In the first quarto (1603) we find a passage indicating most clearly that the events of this act take place on the same day. After Hamlet has left the churchyard with Horatio, the King says to Laertes :—

> " This very day shall Hamlet drinke his last
> For presently we meane to send to him," &c.
>
> (*Allen's Reprint*, p. 90.)

These lines, however, are omitted in all the subsequent editions, and I cannot but think that the omission is remarkable, and goes to support the theory put forward above.

" Sir, I will walk here in the hall ; if it pleases his majesty, it is the breathing time of day with me ; let the foils be brought," &c.

But we may suppose that Hamlet, in saying this, indicates by a gesture the Castle which is close to them, and that he means to say he will attend the King in the hall there.

There is no doubt that this and the subsequent scene were originally played as one, and in the same place ; and that this vague expression *Hall* was used to express a kind of vestibule open on one side to the air. But on the modern stage a change of scene is imperatively necessary ; and it is better to be true to the spirit rather than to the letter of the text.[1]   The last scene

---

[1] Any one who will examine carefully the whole of this scene in the two first quartos and in the first folio, will see that there are many difficulties in arranging it for the stage.   The first quarto (1603), as is often the case, affords the most valuable assistance in determining what was the original intention of Shakespeare. The *Gentleman* who in that edition of the play takes the place of *Osric,* says to *Hamlet :*—

"My lord, presently, the king, and her majesty,
With the rest of the best judgement in the Court,
Are comming downe into the outward pallace."

To which Hamlet answers:—

"Goe tell his majestie, I will attend him."

The *outward pallace* would exactly answer to such a *hall* as has been described above.   But later in the same scene we find Hamlet says :—

"—theres a predestiuate prouidence
In the fall of a sparrow ; heere comes the King."
(See *Allen's Reprint, " the Devonshire Hamlets,"* pp. 94, 95.)

In the second quarto (1604), the text is the same, with the exception of one or two words, as in the ordinary editions of Shakespeare ; but it differs from that of the first folio, for the latter omits altogether lines 182 to 193 inclusive ; or from where *a Lord* enters to where, as marked in the modern editions, he goes out.   It is

takes place in such a "hall" or "vestibule" of the palace as has been alluded to above. Through the arches at the back of the stage are seen the trees of what may be supposed to be the "orchard" in which the good king Hamlet met his death at his brother's hand. The spot is a fitting one for the execution of

worth while to observe what this *Lord* says, addressing Hamlet :—

——" his majesty commended him to you by young Osric
Who brings back to him that you attend him in the hall," &c.
Lines 182, 183.

And again—

"The king and queen and all are coming down."
Line 189.

In the second quarto there is no [*Exit Lord*] marked, so that he probably remained on the scene till the king and queen came on.

At the end of Hamlet's speech commencing,

"Not a whit, we defie augury," &c.

we find in the second quarto the words "Let be," indicating probably that as he saw the king and court approaching, he did not wish to continue the conversation with Horatio. In the second quarto the stage direction which follows is—

A table prepard, Trumpets, Drums and Officers with Cushions, King, Queene, and all the state, Foiles, daggers, and Laertes.

In the first folio it is—

Enter King, Queene, Laertes and Lords, with other Attendants with Foyles, and Gauntlets, a Table and Flagons of Wine on it.

In the first quarto (1603) it is simply—

Enter King, Queene, Leartes, Lords.

From the direction of the second quarto it would seem as if there were a change of scene; from that in the folio, as if the same scene were continued, a conclusion which is confirmed by Hamlet's words:—

"I will walk here in the hall."

On the other hand, the evidence of the first quarto is very con-

that vengeance so long deferred, and the contrast between the soft green foliage of early summer and the
deepening gloom of the tragedy is not inconsistent with
that terrible irony of fate which is one of the leading
characteristics of the story of Hamlet.

With regard to the archæology and to the dresses,
no attempt has been made to obtain any exactness,
which is, from the nature of the play, impossible.   The
characters in Hamlet talk and think like characters of
Shakespeare's own time.   The period in which the
play is supposed to take place is almost fabulous, and
the constant reference to such comparatively modern
implements as "partisans," "cannons," "rapiers," and
"hangers," would render all attempts to reproduce any
one period of Danish history inconsistent with the
spirit of the play exactly in proportion to their accuracy.
Shakespeare does not seem to have aimed at infusing
any "local colouring" into this play as he has in the
case of Macbeth and others.   He has even ignored the
very nature of the country in which he has laid his
scene ; for there are no cliffs at Elsinore which "beetle
o'er their base into the sea."   No formal respect for
geographical or historical accuracy ever hampered
Shakespeare, when the dramatic effect of the situa-
tion, or the poetical vigour of the description was in
question.

The text of this acting edition of Hamlet has been
carefully revised by Mr. Irving.   It will be found to
differ slightly from that used by him on the first production of the play at the Lyceum Theatre (Oct. 30th,
1874), when Mr. Irving played Hamlet for two hundred

flicting, and that of the second quarto doubtful; for it is to be
observed that Hamlet does not say "in *this* hall," nor does the
lord, who comes from the king, say to Hamlet, Osric "brings
back" to the king "that you attend him *here*," but "*in the hall.*"
The omission of the word *Exeunt*, at the end of Hamlet's speech,
would seem, however, to decide the question, as far as the old
copies are concerned, in favour of the continuance of the same
scene.

consecutive nights : the alterations introduced have
been made in accordance with the experience gained
then, and by many later representations of the character
of Hamlet. Whenever any departure has been made
from the text of the 'Cambridge' Shakespeare (edited
by W. G. Clark and W. Aldis Wright), on which this
edition is based, it will be found that the authority for
such departure is one of the three independent early editions of the play; viz., the two first quartos (1603 and
1604) and the first folio (1623). Mr. Irving has endea-
voured to select what is best in each, and to retain as
much as possible of Shakespeare's play in the representation. It is to be hoped that, both in what has been
retained and in what has been omitted, a wise discretion has been exercised ; and that the effectiveness
of this grand tragedy as an acting play has been
increased rather than diminished. Many persons
find the ordinary acting editions of Hamlet too
long, whilst others, in their enthusiasm for the poet's
text, clamour for more of the omitted passages to be
restored. The former must be content to exercise
their patience, and the latter their self-denial. As it
is, the play occupies nearly four hours in representation,
and there is no greater proof of the advance Shakespeare has made in the respect and admiration of our
countrymen, than the fact that audiences, who are so
intolerant, now-a-days, of anything like lengthiness in
modern plays, are willing to sit through the whole of
so long a performance.

F. A. M.

Note.—The references to the numbers of the various lines of
the play quoted in this preface are to the 'Clarendon Press'
Edition of Hamlet.

DRAMATIS PERSONÆ.

CLAUDIUS, King of Denmark . . .		MR. FORRESTER.
HAMLET, son to the late, and nephew to the present King		MR. IRVING.
POLONIUS, Lord Chamberlain . . .		MR. C. COOPER.
LAERTES, son to Polonius		MR. F. COOPER.
HORATIO, friend to Hamlet		MR. FORRESTER.
OSRIC,	Courtiers	MR. J. H. BARNES.
ROSENCRANTZ,		MR. ELWOOD.
GUILDENSTERN,		MR. PINERO.
MARCELLUS,	Officers	MR. TAPPING.
BERNARDO,		MR. GANTHONY.
FRANCISCO, a Soldier		MR. HARWOOD.
REYNALDO		MR. CALVERT.
1st Player		MR. BEAUMONT.
2nd Player		MR. EVERARD.
Priest		MR. COLLETT.
Messenger		MR. RUSSELL.
1st Gravedigger		MR. S. JOHNSON.
2nd Gravedigger		MR. A. ANDREWS.
GHOST of Hamlet's Father		MR. MEAD.
GERTRUDE, Queen of Denmark, and mother to Hamlet		MISS PAUNCEFORT.
OPHELIA, daughter to Polonius . .		MISS ELLEN TERRY.
Player Queen		MISS HARWOOD.

Lords——Ladies——Officers——Soldiers——
Messengers——and other attendants.

SCENE: *Elsinore.*

SYNOPSIS OF SCENERY.

ACT I.

Scene 1. Elsinore—a Platform before the Castle.

Scene 2. A Room of State in the Castle.

Scene 3. A Room in Polonius's House.

Scene 4. The Platform.

Scene 5. A more remote Part.

ACT II.

Scene 1. A Room in Polonius's House.

Scene 2. A Room of State in the Castle.

ACT III.

Scene 1. The same.

Scene 2. A Room in the Castle.

Scene 3. Another Room in the same.

ACT IV.

Scene 1. A Room of State in the Castle.

ACT V.

Scene 1. A Church Yard.

Scene 2. Outside the Castle.

Scene 3. A Hall in the Castle.

HAMLET,

PRINCE OF DENMARK.

ACT I.

SCENE I. *Elsinore. A platform before the castle.*

FRANCISCO *at his post. Enter to him* BERNARDO.

Bernardo.

HO'S there?

Fran. Nay, answer me : stand, and unfold
  yourself.

Ber. Long live the king!

Fran. Bernardo?

Ber. He.

Fran. You come most carefully upon your hour.

Ber. 'Tis now struck twelve ; get thee to bed, Francisco.

Fran. For this relief much thanks : 'tis bitter cold,
And I am sick at heart.

 Ber. Have you had quiet guard?

 Fran.   Not a mouse stirring.

 Ber. Well, good night.
If you do meet Horatio and Marcellus,
The rivals of my watch, bid them make haste.

 Fran. I think I hear them. Stand, ho! Who is
  there?

Enter HORATIO *and* MARCELLUS.

Hor. Friends to this ground.

Mar.   And liegemen to the Dane.

Fran. Give you good night.

Mar.   O, farewell, honest soldier:
Who hath relieved you?

Fran.   Bernardo hath my place.
Give you good night.   [*Exit.*

Mar.   Holla! Bernardo!

Ber.   Say,
What, is Horatio there?

Hor.   A piece of him.

Ber. Welcome, Horatio: welcome, good Marcellus.

Mar. What, has this thing appear'd again to-night?

Ber. I have seen nothing.

Mar. Horatio says, 'tis but our fantasy,
And will not let belief take hold of him
Touching this dreaded sight, twice seen of us:
Therefore I have entreated him along
With us to watch the minutes of this night,
That if again this apparition come,
He may approve our eyes and speak to it.

Hor. Tush, tush, 'twill not appear.

Ber. Come, let us once again assail your ears,
That are so fortified against our story,
What we have two nights seen.

Hor. Well, let us hear Bernardo speak of this.

Ber. Last night of all,
When yond same star that's westward from the pole
Had made his course to illume that part of heaven
Where now it burns, Marcellus and myself,
The bell then beating one,—

Enter Ghost.

Mar. Peace, break thee off; look where it comes
    again!

Ber. In the same figure, like the king that's dead.

Hor. Most like: it harrows me with fear and wonder.

Ber. It would be spoke to.

Mar.   Question it, Horatio.

Hor. What art thou, that usurp'st this time of night,
Together with that fair and warlike form
In which the majesty of buried Denmark
Did sometimes march? by heaven I charge thee, speak!

Mar. It is offended.

Ber.   See, it stalks away!

Hor. Stay! speak, speak! I charge thee speak!

                              [*Exit Ghost.*

Mar. 'Tis gone, and will not answer.

Ber. How now, Horatio! you tremble and look pale:
Is not this something more than fantasy?
What think you on't?

Hor. Before my God, I might not this believe
Without the sensible and true avouch
Of mine own eyes.

Mar. Is it not like the king?

Hor. As thou art to thyself:
Such was the very armour he had on
When he the ambitious Norway combated.

Mar. Thus twice before, and jump at this dead hour,
With martial stalk hath he gone by our watch.

Hor. In what particular thought to work I know not;
But, in the gross and scope of my opinion,
This bodes some strange eruption to our state.

Re-enter Ghost.

But soft, behold! lo, where it comes again!
I'll cross it, though it blast me.   Stay, illusion!
If thou hast any sound, or use of voice,
Speak to me:
If there be any good thing to be done,
That may to thee do ease and grace to me,
Speak to me:
If thou art privy to thy country's fate,
Which, happily, foreknowing may avoid,
O, speak!
Or if thou hast uphoarded in thy life

Extorted treasure in the womb of earth,
For which, they say, you spirits oft walk in death,
Speak of it: stay, and speak! Stop it, Marcellus.

Mar. Shall I strike at it with my partisan?

Hor. Do, if it will not stand.

Ber.   'Tis here!

Hor.   'Tis here!

Mar. 'Tis gone!   *[Exit Ghost.*
We do it wrong, being so majestical,
To offer it the show of violence.

Ber. It was about to speak, when the cock crew.

Hor. And then it started like a guilty thing
Upon a fearful summons. I have heard,
The cock, that is the trumpet to the morn,
Doth with his lofty and shrill-sounding throat
Awake the god of day; and at his warning,
Whether in sea or fire, in earth or air,
The extravagant and erring spirit hies
To his confine.

Mar. Some say that ever 'gainst that season comes
Wherein our Saviour's birth is celebrated,
The bird of dawning singeth all night long:
And then, they say, no spirit dare stir abroad,
The nights are wholesome, then no planets strike,
No fairy takes nor witch hath power to charm,
So hallow'd and so gracious is the time.

Hor. So have I heard and do in part believe it.
But look, the morn, in russet mantle clad,
Walks o'er the dew of yon high eastward hill:
Break we our watch up; and by my advice,
Let us impart what we have seen to-night
Unto young Hamlet; for, upon my life,
The spirit, dumb to us, will speak to him.   *[Exeunt.*

Scene II. *A room of state in the castle.*

Danish March.

Enter the King, Queen, Hamlet, Polonius,
Laertes, Lords, *and* Attendants.

King.

THOUGH yet of Hamlet our dear brother's
death
The memory be green, and that it us befitted
To bear our hearts in grief and our whole kingdom,
To be contracted in one brow of woe,
Yet so far hath discretion fought with nature
That we with wisest sorrow think on him,
Together with remembrance of ourselves.
Therefore our sometime sister, now our queen,
The imperial jointress to this warlike state,
Have we, as 'twere with a defeated joy,
Taken to wife: nor have we herein barr'd
Your better wisdoms, which have freely gone
With this affair along. For all, our thanks.
And now, Laertes, what's the news with you?
You told us of some suit; what is't, Laertes?
    Laer.   Dread my lord,
Your leave and favour to return to France;
From whence though willingly I came to Denmark,
To show my duty in your coronation,
Yet now, I must confess, that duty done,
My thoughts and wishes bend again toward France,
And bow them to your gracious leave and pardon.
    King. Have you your father's leave? What says
        Polonius?
    Pol. He hath, my lord, wrung from me my slow
        leave
By laboursome petition, and at last
Upon his will I seal'd my hard consent:
I do beseech you, give him leave to go.
    King. Take thy fair hour, Laertes; time be thine,

And thy best graces spend it at thy will!
But now, my cousin Hamlet, and my son,—

   Ham. [*Aside*] A little more than kin, and less than
     kind.

   King. How is it that the clouds still hang on you?

   Ham. Not so, my lord: I am too much i' the sun.

   Queen. Good Hamlet, cast thy nighted colour off,
And let thine eye look like a friend on Denmark.
Do not for ever with thy vailed lids
Seek for thy noble father in the dust:
Thou know'st 'tis common; all that live must die,
Passing through nature to eternity.

   Ham. Ay, madam, it is common.

   Queen.   If it be,
Why seems it so particular with thee?

   Ham. Seems, madam? nay, it is; I know not
     "seems."
'Tis not alone my inky cloak, good mother,
Nor customary suits of solemn black,
No, nor the fruitful river in the eye,
Nor the dejected haviour of the visage,
Together with all forms, moods, shapes of grief,
That can denote me truly: these indeed seem,
For they are actions that a man might play:
But I have that within which passeth show;
These but the trappings and the suits of woe.

   King. 'Tis sweet and commendable in your nature,
     Hamlet,
To give these mourning duties to your father:
But, you must know, your father lost a father,
That father lost, lost his, and the survivor bound
In filial obligation for some term
To do obsequious sorrow: but to persever
In obstinate condolement is a course
Of impious stubbornness; 'tis unmanly grief:
It shows a will most incorrect to heaven.
We pray you, throw to earth
This unprevailing woe, and think of us
As of a father: for let the world take note,

You are the most immediate to our throne;
Our chiefest courtier, cousin, and our son.

   Queen. Let not thy mother lose her prayers, Hamlet:
I pray thee, stay with us; go not to Wittenberg.

   Ham. I shall in all my best obey you, madam.

   King. Why, 'tis a loving and a fair reply:
Be as ourself in Denmark. Madam, come;
This gentle and unforced accord of Hamlet
Sits smiling to my heart: in grace whereof,
No jocund health that Denmark drinks to-day,
But the great cannon to the clouds shall tell,
And the king's rouse the heavens shall bruit again,
Re-speaking earthly thunder.

                     [Exeunt all but Hamlet.

   Ham. O, that this too too solid flesh would melt,
Thaw and resolve itself into a dew!
Or that the Everlasting had not fix'd
His canon 'gainst self-slaughter! O God! God!
How weary, stale, flat and unprofitable
Seem to me all the uses of this world!
Fie on't! oh fie! 'tis an unweeded garden
That grows to seed; things rank and gross in nature
Possess it merely. That it should come to this!
But two months dead! nay, not so much, not two:
So excellent a king; that was, to this,
Hyperion to a satyr; so loving to my mother
That he might not beteem the winds of heaven
Visit her face too roughly. Heaven and earth!
Must I remember? why, she would hang on him,
As if increase of appetite had grown
By what it fed on: and yet, within a month,—
Let me not think on't—Frailty, thy name is woman!—
A little month, or ere those shoes were old
With which she follow'd my poor father's body,
Like Niobe, all tears, why she, even she—
O God! a beast that wants discourse of reason,
Would have mourn'd longer—married with mine uncle,
My father's brother, but no more like my father
Than I to Hercules: within a month?

Ere yet the salt of most unrighteous tears
Had left the flushing in her galled eyes,
She married.   O, most wicked speed, to post
With such dexterity to incestuous sheets!
It is not nor it cannot come to good:
But break my heart, for I must hold my tongue.

Enter HORATIO, MARCELLUS, *and* BERNARDO.

Hor. Hail to your lordship!
Ham.   I am glad to see you well:
Horatio,—or I do forget myself.
   Hor. The same, my lord, and your poor servant
        ever.
   Ham. Sir, my good friend; I'll change that name
        with you:
And what make you from Wittenberg, Horatio?
Marcellus?
   Mar. My good lord—
   Ham. I am very glad to see you.   Good even, sir.
But what, in faith, make you from Wittenberg?
   Hor. A truant disposition, good my lord.
   Ham. I would not hear your enemy say so,
Nor shall you do mine ear that violence,
To make it truster of your own report
Against yourself: I know you are no truant.
But what is your affair in Elsinore?
We'll teach you to drink deep ere you depart.
   Hor. My lord, I came to see your father's funeral.
   Ham. I pray thee, do not mock me, fellow-student;
I think it was to see my mother's wedding.
   Hor. Indeed, my lord, it follow'd hard upon.
   Ham. Thrift, thrift, Horatio! the funeral baked-
        meats
Did coldly furnish forth the marriage tables.
Would I had met my dearest foe in heaven
Or ever I had seen that day, Horatio!
My father!—methinks I see my father.
   Hor. O where, my lord?

Ham. In my mind's eye, Horatio.

Hor. I saw him once ; he was a goodly king.

Ham. He was a man, take him for all in all,
I shall not look upon his like again.

Hor. My lord, I think I saw him yesternight.

Ham. Saw ? who ?

Hor. My lord, the king your father.

Ham. The king my father !

Hor. Season your admiration for a while
With an attent ear, till I may deliver,
Upon the witness of these gentlemen,
This marvel to you.

Ham. For God's love, let me hear.

Hor. Two nights together had these gentlemen,
Marcellus and Bernardo, on their watch,
In the dead vast and middle of the night,
Been thus encounter'd. A figure like your father,
Armed at point exactly, cap-a-pe,
Appears before them, and with solemn march
Goes slow and stately by them : thrice he walk'd
By their oppress'd and fear-surprised eyes,
Within his truncheon's length ; whilst they, bestil'd
Almost to jelly with the act of fear,
Stand dumb, and speak not to him. This to me
In dreadful secrecy impart they did ;
And I with them the third night kept the watch :
Where, as they had deliver'd, both in time,
Form of the thing, each word made true and good,
The apparition comes : I knew your father ;
These hands are not more like.

Ham. But where was this ?

Mar. My lord, upon the platform where we watch'd.

Ham. Did you not speak to it ?

Hor. My lord, I did ;
But answer made it none : yet once methought
It lifted up its head and did address
Itself to motion, like as it would speak ;
But even then the morning cock crew loud,
And at the sound it shrunk in haste away,

And vanish'd from our sight.

Ham.   'Tis very strange.

Hor. As I do live, my honour'd lord, 'tis true;
And we did think it writ down in our duty
To let you know of it.

Ham. Indeed, indeed, sirs, but this troubles me.
Hold you the watch to-night?

Mar.   We do, my lord.

Ham. Arm'd, say you?

Mar. Arm'd, my lord.

Ham. From top to toe?

Mar.   My lord, from head to foot.

Ham. Then saw you not his face?

Hor. O, yes, my lord; he wore his beaver up.

Ham. What, look'd he frowningly?

Hor. A countenance more in sorrow than in anger.

Ham. Pale, or red?

Hor. Nay, very pale.

Ham.   And fix'd his eyes upon you?

Hor. Most constantly.

Ham.   I would I had been there.

Hor. It would have much amazed you.

Ham. Very like, very like.   Stay'd it long?

Hor. While one with moderate haste might tell
      a hundred.

Mar. ⎫
Ber. ⎬ Longer, longer.

Hor. Not when I saw't.

Ham.   His beard was grizzled? no?

Hor. It was, as I have seen it in his life,
A sable silver'd.

Ham.   I'll watch to-night; perchance 'twill
      walk again.

Hor.   I warrant you it will.

Ham. If it assume my noble father's person,
I'll speak to it, though hell itself should gape
And bid me hold my peace. I pray you all,
If you have hitherto conceal'd this sight,
Let it be tenable in your silence still;

And whatsoever else shall hap to-night,
Give it an understanding, but no tongue :
I will requite your loves.   So, fare ye well :
Upon the platform, 'twixt eleven and twelve,
I'll visit you.
    All.   Our duty to your honour.
    Ham. Your love, as mine to you : farewell.
                        [Exeunt all but Hamlet.
My father's spirit in arms ! all is not well ;
I doubt some foul play : would the night were come !
Till then sit still, my soul : foul deeds will rise,
Though all the earth o'erwhelm them to men's eyes.
                             [Exit.

Scene III.   *A room in Polonius's house.*

Enter Laertes *and* Ophelia.

Laertes.

M Y necessaries are embark'd : farewell :
    And, sister, as the winds give benefit,
    Pray let me hear from you.
    Oph.   Do you doubt that ?
    Laer. For Hamlet and the trifling of his favour,
Hold it a fashion and a toy in blood :
He may not, as unvalued persons do,
Carve for himself, for on his choice depends
The safety and health of this whole state ;
Then weigh what loss your honour may sustain,
If with too credent ear you list his songs :
Fear it, Ophelia, fear it, my dear sister,
The chariest maid is prodigal enough,
If she unmask her beauty to the moon.
    Oph. I shall the effect of this good lesson keep,
As watchman to my heart.   But, good my brother,

Do not, as some ungracious pastors do,
Show me the steep and thorny way to heaven ;
Whiles, like a puff'd and reckless libertine,
Himself the primrose path of dalliance treads
And recks not his own rede.
　Laer.　　　　　　　O, fear me not.
I stay too long : but here my father comes.

Enter POLONIUS.

　Pol. Yet here, Laertes ! aboard, aboard, for shame!
The wind sits in the shoulder of your sail,
And you are stay'd for.　There; my blessing with
　　　thee !
And these few precepts in thy memory
Look thou character.　Give thy thoughts no tongue,
Nor any unproportion'd thought his act.
Be thou familiar, but by no means vulgar.
Those friends thou hast, and their adoption tried,
Grapple them to thy soul with hoops of steel,
But do not dull thy palm with entertainment
Of each new-hatch'd, unfledged comrade.　Beware
Of entrance to a quarrel, but being in,
Bear't that the opposed may beware of thee.
Give every man thy ear, but few thy voice :
Take each man's censure, but reserve thy judgment.
Costly thy habit as thy purse can buy,
But not express'd in fancy ; rich, not gaudy ;
For the apparel oft proclaims the man,
And they in France of the best rank and station
Are of a most select and generous chief in that.
Neither a borrower nor a lender be ;
For loan oft loses both itself and friend,
And borrowing dulls the edge of husbandry.
This above all : to thine ownself be true,
And it must follow, as the night the day,
Thou canst not then be false to any man.
Farewell : my blessing season this in thee !
　Laer. Most humbly do I take my leave, my lord.

Pol. The time invites you; go; your servants tend.

Laer. Farewell, Ophelia, and remember well
What I have said to you.

Oph.   'Tis in my memory lock'd,
And you yourself shall keep the key of it.

Laer. Farewell.   [*Exit.*

Pol. What is't, Ophelia, he hath said to you?

Oph. So please you, something touching the Lord
Hamlet.

Pol. Marry, well bethought:
'Tis told me, he hath very oft of late
Given private time to you, and you yourself
Have of your audience been most free and bounteous:
If it be so—as so 'tis put on me,
And that in way of caution—I must tell you,
You do not understand yourself so clearly
As it behoves my daughter and your honour.
What is between you? give me up the truth.

Oph. He hath, my lord, of late made many tenders
Of his affection to me.

Pol. Affection! pooh! you speak like a green girl,
Unsifted in such perilous circumstance.
Do you believe his tenders, as you call them?

Oph. I do not know, my lord, what I should think.

Pol. Marry, I'll teach you: think yourself a baby,
That you have ta'en these tenders for true pay,
Which are not sterling. Tender yourself more dearly;
Or you'll tender me a fool.

Oph. My lord, he hath importuned me with love
In honourable fashion.

Pol. Ay, fashion you may call it; go to, go to.

Oph. And hath given countenance to his speech,
my lord,
With almost all the holy vows of heaven.

Pol. Ay, springes to catch woodcocks. I do know,
When the blood burns, how prodigal the soul
Lends the tongue vows. This is for all:
I would not, in plain terms, from this time forth,
Have you so slander any moment leisure,

As to give words or talk with the Lord Hamlet.
Look to't, I charge you : come your ways.

    Oph. I shall obey, my lord.   [*Exeunt*

SCENE IV. *The platform.*

Enter HAMLET *and* HORATIO, *to* MARCELLUS, *who is
on guard.*

Hamlet.

THE air bites shrewdly ; it is very cold.

    Hor. It is a nipping and an eager air.

    Ham. What hour now ?

  Hor.   I think it lacks of twelve.

  Mar. No, it is struck.

  Hor. Indeed ? I heard it not : it then draws near
    the season
Wherein the spirit held his wont to walk,

    [*A flourish of trumpets : Ordnance shot off within.*
What does this mean, my lord ?

  Ham. The king doth wake to-night and takes his
    rouse,
Keeps wassail, and the swaggering up-spring reels ;
And, as he drains his draughts of Rhenish down,
The kettle-drum and trumpet thus bray out
The triumph of his pledge.

  Hor.   Is it a custom ?

  Ham. Ay, marry, is 't :
But to my mind, though I am native here
And to the manner born, it is a custom
More honour'd in the breach than the observance.

Enter Ghost.

  Hor.   Look, my lord, it comes !

  Ham. Angels and ministers of grace defend us !
Be thou a spirit of health or goblin damn'd,
Bring with thee airs from heaven or blasts from hell,

Be thy intents wicked or charitable,
Thou comest in such a questionable shape
That I will speak to thee : I'll call thee Hamlet,
King, father ; Royal Dane, O, answer me !
Let me not burst in ignorance ; but tell
Why thy canonized bones, hearsed in death,
Have burst their cerements ; why the sepulchre,
Wherein we saw thee quietly inurn'd,
Hath oped his ponderous and marble jaws,
To cast thee up again.   What may this mean,
That thou, dead corse, again in complete steel
Revisit'st thus the glimpses of the moon,
Making night hideous ; and we fools of nature
So horridly to shake our disposition
With thoughts beyond the reaches of our souls ?
Say, why is this ? wherefore ? what should we do ?

 Hor. It beckons you to go away with it,
As if it some impartment did desire
To you alone.

 Mar. Look, with what courteous action
It waves you to a more removed ground :
But do not go with it.

 Hor.   No, by no means.

 Ham. It will not speak ; then will I follow it.

 Hor. Do not, my lord.

 Ham.   Why, what should be the fear ?
I do not set my life at a pin's fee ;
And for my soul, what can it do to that,
Being a thing immortal as itself ?
It waves me forth again : I'll follow it.

 Hor. What if it tempt you toward the flood, my
  lord,
Or to the dreadful summit of the cliff,
And there assume some other horrible form,
And draw you into madness ?

 Ham.   It wafts me still.
Go on ; I'll follow thee.

 Mar. You shall not go, my lord.

 Ham.   Hold off your hands.

Hor. Be ruled; you shall not go.
Ham.   My fate cries out,
And makes each petty artery in this body
As hardy as the Nemean lion's nerve.
Still am I call'd :—unhand me, gentlemen.
By heaven, I'll make a ghost of him that lets me :
I say, away!   Go on ; I'll follow thee.

> [*Exeunt Ghost and Hamlet, followed by*
> *Horatio and Marcellus.*

SCENE V.   *A more remote part.*

Enter Ghost *and* HAMLET.

Hamlet.

HITHER wilt thou lead me? speak, I'll go
no further.
    Ghost. Mark me.
Ham.   I will.
Ghost.   My hour is almost come,
When I to sulphurous and tormenting flames
Must render up myself.
Ham.   Alas, poor ghost!
Ghost. Pity me not, but lend thy serious hearing
To what I shall unfold.
Ham.   Speak ; I am bound to hear.
Ghost. So art thou to revenge, when thou shalt hear.
Ham. What ?
Ghost. I am thy father's spirit ;
Doom'd for a certain term to walk the night,
And for the day confined to fast in fires,
Till the foul crimes done in my days of nature
Are burnt and purged away.   But that I am forbid
To tell the secrets of my prison-house,
I could a tale unfold whose lightest word
Would harrow up thy soul, freeze thy young blood,
Make thy two eyes, like stars, start from their spheres,
Thy knotted and combined locks to part

And each particular hair to stand on end,
Like quills upon the fretful porcupine:
But this eternal blazon must not be
To ears of flesh and blood. List, list, O, list!
If thou didst ever thy dear father love—

Ham. O God!

Ghost. Revenge his foul and most unnatural murder.

Ham. Murder!

Ghost. Murder most foul, as in the best it is;
But this most foul, strange and unnatural.

Ham. Haste me to know't, that I, with wings as swift
As meditation or the thoughts of love,
May sweep to my revenge.

Ghost.   I find thee apt;
Now, Hamlet, hear:
'Tis given out that, sleeping in my orchard,
A serpent stung me; so the whole ear of Denmark
Is by a forged process of my death
Rankly abused: but know, thou noble youth,
The serpent that did sting thy father's life
Now wears his crown.

Ham.   O my prophetic soul!
Mine uncle!

Ghost. Ay, that incestuous, that adulterate beast,
With witchcraft of his wit, with traitorous gifts,—
Won to his shameful lust
The will of my most seeming-virtuous queen:
O Hamlet, what a falling-off was there!
From me, whose love was of that dignity
That it went hand in hand even with the vow
I made to her in marriage, and to decline
Upon a wretch whose natural gifts were poor
To those of mine!
But, soft! methinks I scent the morning air;
Brief let me be. Sleeping within mine orchard,
My custom always of the afternoon,
Upon my secure hour thy uncle stole,
With juice of cursed hebenon in a vial,
And in the porches of my ears did pour

The leperous distilment; whose effect
Holds such an enmity with blood of man
That swift as quicksilver it courses through
The natural gates and alleys of the body.
So did it mine.
Thus was I, sleeping, by a brother's hand
Of life, of crown, of queen, at once dispatch'd ;
Cut off even in the blossoms of my sin,
No reckoning made, but sent to my account
With all my imperfections on my head.
    Ham. O, horrible ! O, horrible ! most horrible !
    Ghost. If thou hast nature in thee, bear it not ;
Let not the royal bed of Denmark be
A couch for luxury and damned incest.
But, howsoever thou pursuest this act,
Taint not thy mind, nor let thy soul contrive
Against thy mother aught : leave her to heaven
And to those thorns that in her bosom lodge,
To prick and sting her.   Fare thee well at once !
The glow-worm shows the matin to be near,
And 'gins to pale his uneffectual fire :
Adieu, adieu, adieu ! remember me.   [*Exit.*
    Ham. O all you host of heaven! O earth! what else ?
And shall I couple hell ? O fie ! Hold, hold, my heart;
And you, my sinews, grow not instant old,
But bear me stiffly up.   Remember thee !
Ay, thou poor ghost, while memory holds a seat
In this distracted globe.   Remember thee !
Yea, from the table of my memory
I'll wipe away all trivial fond records,
All saws of books, all forms, all pressures past,
That youth and observation copied there ;
And thy commandment all alone shall live
Within the book and volume of my brain,
Unmix'd with baser matter : yes, by heaven !
O most pernicious woman !
O villain, villain, smiling, damned villain !
My tables, my tables,—meet it is I set it down,
That one may smile, and smile, and be a villain ;

At least I'm sure it may be so in Denmark: [*Writing.*
So, uncle, there you are.   Now to my word ;
It is " Adieu, adieu ! remember me."
I have sworn't.

   Mar. } [*Within*] My lord, my lord !
   Hor. }
   Mar. [*Within*] Lord Hamlet !
   Hor. [*Within*]   Heaven secure him !
   Ham. So be it !
   Hor. [*Within*] Hillo, ho, ho, my lord !
   Ham. Hillo, ho, ho, boy ! come, bird, come.

Enter HORATIO *and* MARCELLUS.

   Mar. How is't, my noble lord ?
   Hor.   What news, my lord ?
   Ham. O ! wonderful !
   Hor. Good my lord, tell it.
   Ham.   No ; you will reveal it.
   Hor. Not I, my lord, by heaven.
   Mar.   Nor I, my lord.
   Ham. How say you, then ; would heart of man once
     think it ?
But you 'll be secret ?
   Hor. }
            Ay, by heaven, my lord.
   Mar. }
   Ham. There's ne'er a villain dwelling in all Denmark—
But he's an arrant knave.
   Hor. There needs no ghost, my lord, come from the
     grave
To tell us this.
   Ham.   Why, right ; you are i' the right ;
And so, without more circumstance at all,
I hold it fit that we shake hands and part :
You, as your business and desire shall point you ;
For every man hath business and desire,
Such as it is ; and for my own poor part,
Look you, I 'll go pray.
   Hor. These are but wild and whirling words, my lord

Ham. I'm sorry they offend you, heartily;
Yes, faith, heartily.

Hor.   There's no offence, my lord.

Ham. Yes, by Saint Patrick, but there is, my lord,
And much offence too.   Touching this vision here,
It is an honest ghost, that let me tell you:
For your desire to know what is between us,
O'ermaster't as you may.   And now, good friends,
As you are friends, scholars and soldiers,
Give me one poor request.

Hor. What is't, my lord? we will.

Ham. Never make known what you have seen to-
    night.

Hor. ⎱
Mar. ⎰ My lord, we will not.

Ham.   Nay, but swear 't.

Hor.   In faith,
My lord, not I.

Mar.   Nor I, my lord, in faith.

Ham. Upon my sword.

Mar.   We have sworn, my lord, already.

Ham. Indeed, upon my sword, indeed.

Ghost. [*Beneath*] Swear.

Ham. Ah, ha, boy! say'st thou so? art thou there,
    truepenny?
Come on: You hear this fellow in the cellarage:
Consent to swear.

Hor. Propose the oath, my lord.

Ham. Never to speak of this that you have seen.
Swear by my sword.

Ghost. [*Beneath*] Swear.

Ham. Hic et ubique? then we'll shift our ground.
Come hither, gentlemen,
And lay your hands again upon my sword,
Never to speak of this that you have heard:
Swear by my sword.

Ghost. [*Beneath*] Swear.

Ham. Well said, old mole! canst work i' the earth
    so fast?

A worthy pioneer! Once more remove, good friends.
　　Hor. O day and night, but this is wondrous strange!
　　Ham. And therefore as a stranger give it welcome.
There are more things in Heaven and earth, Horatio,
Than are dreamt of in our philosophy.
But come;
Here, as before, never, so help you mercy,
How strange or odd soe'er I bear myself,
As I perchance hereafter shall think meet
To put an antic disposition on,
That you, at such times seeing me, never shall,
With arms encumber'd thus, or thus head-shake,
Or by pronouncing of some doubtful phrase,
As "Well, well, we know," or "We could, an if we
　　would,"
Or "If we list to speak," or "There be, an if they might,"
Or such ambiguous giving out, to note
That you know aught of me: this not to do,
So grace and mercy at your most need help you,
Swear.
　　Ghost. [*Beneath*] Swear.
　　Ham. Rest, rest, perturbed spirit! [*They swear*]
　　　　So, gentlemen,
With all my love I do commend me to you:
And what so poor a man as Hamlet is
May do, to express his love and friending to you,
God willing, shall not lack. Let us go in together;
And still your fingers on your lips, I pray.
The time is out of joint: O cursed spite,
That ever I was born to set it right!
Nay, come, let's go together. 　　　　[*Exeunt*

ACT II.

SCENE I. A room in Polonius's house.

Enter POLONIUS and REYNALDO.

Polonius.

 IVE him this money and these notes, Reynaldo.

Rey. I will, my lord.

Pol. You shall do marvellous wisely,
good Reynaldo,
Before you visit him, to make inquire
Of his behaviour.

Rey. My lord, I did intend it.

Pol. Observe his inclination in yourself.

Rey. I shall, my lord.

Pol. And let him ply his music.

Rey. Well, my lord.

Pol. Farewell.

Enter OPHELIA.

How now, Ophelia! what's the matter?

Oph. O, my lord, my lord, I have been so affrighted!

Pol. With what, i' the name of God?

Oph. My lord, as I was sewing in my closet
Lord Hamlet, with his doublet all unbraced;
No hat upon his head;
Pale as his shirt; his knees knocking each other,
And with a look so piteous in purport
As if he had been loosed out of hell
To speak of horrors, he comes before me.

Pol. Mad for thy love?

Oph.   My lord, I do not know ;
But truly I do fear it.
  Pol.   What said he ?
  Oph. He took me by the wrist and held me hard ;
Then goes he to the length of all his arm ;
And with his other hand thus o'er his brow,
He falls to such perusal of my face
As he would draw it.   Long stay'd he so ;
At last, a little shaking of mine arm,
And thrice his head thus waving up and down,
He raised a sigh so piteous and profound
As it did seem to shatter all his bulk
And end his being : that done, he lets me go :
And with his head over his shoulder turn'd,
He seem'd to find his way without his eyes ;
For out o' doors he went without their help,
And to the last bended their light on me.
  Pol. Come, go with me : I will go seek the king.
This is the very ecstasy of love,
Whose violent property fordoes itself
And leads the will to desperate undertakings.
I am sorry.
What, have you given him any hard words of late ?
  Oph. No, my good lord ; but, as you did command,
I did repel his letters and denied
His access to me.
  Pol.   That hath made him mad.
I am sorry that with better heed and judgement
I had not quoted him.
Come, go we to the king :
This must be known ; which, being kept close, might
      move
More grief to hide than hate to utter love.   [*Exeunt.*

SCENE II.   *A room of state in the castle.*

Enter KING, QUEEN, ROSENCRANTZ, GUILDENSTERN,
and Attendants.

King.

WELCOME, dear Rosencrantz and Guilden-
        stern !
        Moreover that we much did long to see you,
The need we have to use you did provoke
Our hasty sending.   Something have you heard
Of Hamlet's transformation ;
What it should be,
More than his father's death, that thus hath put him
So much from the understanding of himself,
I cannot dream of : I entreat you both,
That you vouchsafe your rest here in our court
Some little time : so by your companies
To draw him on to pleasures, and to gather
So much as from occasion you may glean,
Whether aught, to us unknown, afflicts him thus,
That open'd lies within our remedy.
    Queen. Good gentlemen, he hath much talk'd of you ;
And sure I am two men there are not living
To whom he more adheres.   If it will please you
As to expend your time with us awhile,
Your visitation shall receive such thanks
As fits a king's remembrance.
    Ros.   Both your majesties
Might, by the sovereign power you have of us,
Put your dread pleasures more into command
Than to entreaty.
    Guil.   But we both obey,
And here give up ourselves, in the full bent
To lay our service freely at your feet,
To be commanded.
    King. Thanks, Rosencrantz and gentle Guildenstern.
    Queen. Thanks, Guildenstern and gentle Rosen-
        crantz :

And I beseech you instantly to visit
My too much changed son. Go, some of you,
And bring these gentlemen where Hamlet is.
    [*Exeunt Rosencrantz, Guildenstern, and Attendants.*

Enter POLONIUS.

   Pol. I do think, or else this brain of mine
Hunts not the trail of policy so sure
As it hath used to do, that I have found
The very cause of Hamlet's lunacy.
   King. O, speak of that; that do I long to hear.
   Pol. My liege, and madam,
I have a daughter—have while she is mine—
Who, in her duty and obedience, mark,
Hath given me this : now gather and surmise.
    [*Reads*]
   "To the celestial and my soul's idol, the most beau-
tified Ophelia,"—
That's an ill phrase, a vile phrase; "beautified" is a
vile phrase : but you shall hear. Thus :
    [*Reads*]
   "In her excellent white bosom, these, &c."
   Queen. Came this from Hamlet to her ?
   Pol. Good Madam, stay awhile; I will be faithful.
    [*Reads*]
        "Doubt thou the stars are fire ;
         Doubt that the sun doth move ;
        Doubt truth to be a liar ;
         But never doubt I love.
   "O dear Ophelia, I am ill at these numbers ; I have
not art to reckon my groans : but that I love thee
best, O most best, believe it. Adieu.
        "Thine evermore, most dear lady,
           whilst this machine is to him,
                HAMLET."
This in obedience hath my daughter shown me,
And I went round to work,
And my young mistress thus I did bespeak :

"Lord Hamlet is a prince, out of thy star ;
This must not be:" and then I prescripts gave her,
That she should lock herself from his resort,
Admit no messengers, receive no tokens.
Which done, she took the fruits of my advice ;
And he repulsed, a short tale to make,
Fell into a sadness, then into a fast,
Thence to a watch, thence into a weakness,
Thence to a lightness, and by this declension
Into the madness wherein now he raves
And all we mourn for.

    King. Do you think 'tis this ?

    Queen.   It may be, very like.

    Pol. Hath there been such a time, I'd fain know that,
That I have positively said " 'Tis so,"
When it proved otherwise ?

    King.   Not that I know.

    Pol. [*pointing to his head and shoulder*] Take this
         from this, if this be otherwise :
If circumstances lead me, I will find
Where truth is hid, though it were hid indeed
Within the centre.

    King.   How may we try it further ?

    Pol. You know, sometimes he walks four hours
         together
Here in the lobby.

    Queen.   So he does indeed.

    Pol. At such a time I'll loose my daughter to him :
Be you and I behind an arras then ;
Mark the encounter : if he love her not,
And be not from his reason fall'n thereon,
Let me be no assistant for a state,
But keep a farm and carters.

    King.   We will try it.

    Queen. But look where sadly the poor wretch comes
         reading.

    Pol. Away, I do beseech you, both away :
I'll board him presently.

                  [*Exeunt King, Queen, and Attendants.*

Enter HAMLET, *reading.*

How does my good Lord Hamlet ?

Ham. Well, God-a-mercy.

Pol. Do you know me, my lord ?

Ham. Excellent, excellent well; y' are a fishmonger.

Pol. Not I, my lord.

Ham. Then I would you were so honest a man.

Pol. Honest, my lord !

Ham. Ay, sir; to be honest, as this world goes, is to be one man picked out of ten thousand.

Pol. That's very true, my lord.

Ham. [*Reads*] " For if the sun breed maggots in a dead dog, being a good kissing carrion "—Have you a daughter ?

Pol. I have, my lord.

Ham. Let her not walk i' the sun : conception is a blessing ; but not as your daughter may conceive,— friend, look to't.

Pol. [*Aside*] How say you by that ? Still harping on my daughter : yet he knew me not at first ; he said I was a fishmonger : he is far gone, far gone. I'll speak to him again. What do you read, my lord ?

Ham. Words, words, words.

Pol. What is the matter, my lord ?

Ham. Between who ?

Pol. I mean, the matter that you read, my lord.

Ham. Slanders, sir : for the satirical rogue says here that old men have grey beards, that their faces are wrinkled, their eyes purging thick amber and plum-tree gum, and that they have a plentiful lack of wit, together with most weak hams : all which, sir, though I most powerfully and potently believe, yet I hold it not honesty to have it thus set down ; for yourself, sir, should be old as I am, if like a crab you could go backward.

Pol. [*Aside*] Though this be madness, yet there is method in 't. Will you walk out of the air, my lord ?

Ham. Into my grave ?

Pol. Indeed, that is out o' the air. [*Aside*] How pregnant sometimes his replies are! a happiness that often madness hits on, which reason and sanity could not so prosperously be delivered of. I will leave him, and suddenly contrive the means of meeting between him and my daughter.—My honourable lord, I will most humbly take my leave of you.

Ham. You cannot, sir, take from me anything that I will more willingly part withal : except my life, except my life, except my life.

Pol. Fare you well, my lord.   [*Exit.*

Ham. These tedious old fools.

Pol.⎱   You go to seek the Lord Hamlet;
      ⎰ [*Without*]   there he is.
Ros.⎱   [*To Pol.*] God save you, sir!

Enter ROSENCRANTZ *and* GUILDENSTERN.

Guil. My honoured lord!

Ros. My most dear lord!

Ham. My excellent good friends! How dost thou, Guildenstern? Oh, Rosencrantz : good lads : how do you both? What news?

Ros. None, my lord, but that the world's grown honest.

Ham. Then is doomsday near : but your news is not true. What have you, my good friends, deserved at the hands of Fortune, that she sends you to prison hither?

Guil. Prison, my lord?

Ham. Denmark's a prison.

Ros. We think not so, my lord.

Ham. Why, then 'tis none to you; for there is nothing either good or bad, but thinking makes it so : to me it is a prison.

Ros. Why, then your ambition makes it one; 'tis too narrow for your mind.

Ham. O God, I could be bounded in a nut-shell and count myself a king of infinite space, were it not that I have bad dreams.

Guil. Which dreams indeed are ambition ; for the very substance of the ambitious is merely the shadow of a dream.

Ham. A dream itself is but a shadow.

Ros. Truly, and I hold ambition of so airy and light a quality that it is but a shadow's shadow.

Ham. Then are our beggars bodies, and our monarchs and outstretched heroes the beggars' shadows. Shall we to the court ? for, by my fay, I cannot reason.

Ros. }
Guil. } We'll wait upon you.

Ham. No such matter : I will not sort you with the rest of my servants ; for, to speak to you like an honest man, I am most dreadfully attended. But, in the beaten way of friendship, what make you at Elsinore ?

Ros. To visit you, my lord ; no other occasion.

Ham. Beggar that I am, I am even poor in thanks ; but I thank you : and sure, dear friends, my thanks are too dear a halfpenny. Were you not sent for ? Is it your own inclining ? Is it a free visitation ? Come, deal justly with me : come, come ; nay, speak.

Guil. What should we say, my lord ?

Ham. Why, any thing, but to the purpose. You were sent for ; and there is a kind of confession in your looks which your modesties have not craft enough to colour : I know the good king and queen have sent for you.

Ros. To what end, my lord ?

Ham. That you must teach me. But let me conjure you, by the rights of our fellowship, by the consonancy of our youth, by the obligation of our ever-preserved love, and by what more dear a better proposer could charge you withal, be even and direct with me, whether you were sent for, or no.

Ros. [*Aside to Guil.*] What say you ?

Ham. [*Aside*] Nay, then, I have an eye of you.—If you love me, hold not off.

Guil. My lord, we were sent for.

Ham. I will tell you why; so shall my anticipation prevent your discovery, and your secrecy to the king and queen moult no feather. I have of late—but wherefore I know not—lost all my mirth, forgone all custom of exercises ; and indeed it goes so heavily with my disposition that this goodly frame, the earth, seems to me a sterile promontory ; this most excellent canopy, the air, look you, this brave o'erhanging firmament, this majestical roof fretted with golden fire,—why, it appears no other thing to me than a foul and pestilent congregation of vapours. What a piece of work is a man ! how noble in reason ! how infinite in faculty ! in form and moving how express and admirable ! in action how like an angel ! in apprehension how like a god ! the beauty of the world ! the paragon of animals ! And yet, to me, what is this quintessence of dust ? man delights not me—no, nor woman neither, though by your smiling you seem to say so.

Ros. My lord, there was no such stuff in my thoughts.

Ham. Why did you laugh then, when I said " man delights not me ?"

Ros. To think, my lord, if you delight not in man, what lenten entertainment the players shall receive from you : we coted them on the way ; and hither are they coming, to offer you service.

Ham. He that plays the king shall be welcome ; his majesty shall have tribute of me. What players are they ?

Ros. Even those you were wont to take such delight in, the tragedians of the city.

Ham. How chances it they travel ? their residence, both in reputation and in profit, was better both ways. Do they hold the same estimation they did when I was in the city ? are they so followed ?

Ros. No, indeed, are they not.

Ham. It is not very strange ; for my uncle is king

of Denmark, and those that would make mows at him
while my father lived, give twenty, forty, fifty, a hundred ducats a-piece for his picture in little. There is
something in this more than natural, if philosophy
could find it out.   [*Trumpet within.*

Guil. There are the players.

Ham. Gentlemen, you are welcome to Elsinore.
Your hands, come then : the appurtenance of welcome
is fashion and ceremony. You are welcome : but my
uncle-father and aunt-mother are deceived.

Guil. In what, my dear lord ?

Ham. I am but mad north-north-west : when the
wind is southerly I know a hawk from a hernshaw.

Pol. [*Without*] Well be with you, gentlemen !

Ham. Hark you, Guildenstern ; and you too : at
each ear a hearer : that great baby you see there is not
yet out of his swaddling clouts.

Ros. Happily he's the second time come to them ;
for they say an old man is twice a child.

Ham. I will prophesy he comes to tell me of the
players ; mark it. You say right, sir : o' Monday
morning ; 'twas so indeed.

Enter POLONIUS.

Pol. My lord, I have news to tell you.

Ham. My lord, I have news to tell you. When Ros-
cius was an actor in Rome,—

Pol. The actors are come hither, my lord.

Ham. Buz, buz !

Pol. Upon my honour,—

Ham. Then came each actor on his ass,—

Pol. The best actors in the world, either for tragedy,
comedy, history, pastoral, pastoral-comical, historical-
pastoral, tragical-historical, tragical-comical-historical-
pastoral, scene individable, or poem unlimited : Seneca
cannot be too heavy, nor Plautus too light. For the
law of writ and the liberty, these are the only men.

Ham. O Jephthah, judge of Israel, what a treasure hadst thou!

Pol. What a treasure had he, my lord?

Ham. Why,

"One fair daughter and no more,
The which he loved passing well."

Pol. [*Aside*] Still on my daughter.

Ham. Am I not i' the right, old Jephthah?

Pol. If you call me Jephthah, my lord, I have a daughter that I love passing well.

Ham. Nay, that follows not.

Pol. What follows, then, my lord?

Ham. Why,

"As by lot, God wot,"

and then, you know,

"It came to pass, as most like it was,"—

the first row of the pious chanson will show you more; for look, where my abridgement comes.

Enter four or five Players.

You are welcome, masters; welcome all. O, my old friend! thy face is valiant since I saw thee last: comest thou to beard me in Denmark? What, my young lady and mistress! By'r lady, your ladyship is nearer to heaven than when I saw you last, by the altitude of a chopine. You are all welcome. We'll e'en to't like French falconers, fly at anything we see: we'll have a speech straight: come, give us a taste of your quality; come, a passionate speech.

First Play. What speech, my good lord?

Ham. I heard thee speak me a speech once, but it was never acted; or, if it was, not above once; for the play, I remember, pleased not the million; 'twas caviare to the general: but it was an excellent play, well digested in the scenes, set down with as much modesty as cunning. One speech in it I chiefly loved: 'twas

Æneas' tale to Dido ; and thereabout of it especially,
where he speaks of Priam's slaughter : if it live in your
memory, begin at this line :

"The rugged Pyrrhus, like the Hyrcanian beast,"—
It is not so : it begins with "Pyrrhus :" let me see, let
me see ;

"The rugged Pyrrhus, he whose sable arms,
Black as his purpose, did the night resemble
When he lay couched in the ominous horse—
With eyes like carbuncles, the hellish Pyrrhus
Old grandsire Priam seeks."

Pol. 'Fore Heaven, my lord, well spoken, with good
accent and good discretion.

Ham. So !—proceed you.

First Play.   "Anon he finds him
Striking too short at Greeks ; his antique sword,
Rebellious to his arm, lies where it falls,
Repugnant to command : unequal match'd,
Pyrrhus at Priam drives ; in rage strikes wide ;
But with the whiff and wind of his fell sword
The unnerved father falls.
But as we often see, against some storm,
A silence in the heavens, the rack stand still,
The bold winds speechless and the orb below
As hush as death, anon the dreadful thunder
Doth rend the region, so after Pyrrhus' pause
Aroused vengeance sets him new a-work ;
And never did the Cyclops' hammers fall
On Mars's armour, forged for proof eterne,
With less remorse than Pyrrhus' bleeding sword
Now falls on Priam.
Out, out, thou strumpet, Fortune !"

Pol. This is too long.

Ham. It shall to the barber's, with your beard.
Prithee, say on : come to Hecuba.

First Play. "But who, O, who had seen the mobled
     queen—"

Ham. The mobled queen !

Pol. That's good ; "mobled queen" is good.

First Play. " Run barefoot up and down, threatening
     the flames ;
A clout upon that head
Where late the diadem stood ; and for a robe,
A blanket, in the alarm of fear caught up :
Who this had seen, with tongue in venom steep'd
'Gainst Fortune's state would treason have pronounced :
But if the gods themselves did see her then,
When she saw Pyrrhus make malicious sport
In mincing with his sword her husband's limbs,
The instant burst of clamour that she made,
Unless things mortal move them not at all,
Would have made milch the burning eyes of heaven,
And passion in the gods."

Pol. Look, whether he has not turned his colour and
has tears in 's eyes. Prithee, no more.

Ham. 'Tis well ; I'll have thee speak out the rest of
this soon. Good my lord, will you see the players well
bestowed ? Do you hear, let them be well used, for
they are the abstract and brief chronicles of the time :
after your death you were better have a bad epitaph
than their ill report while you live.

Pol. My lord, I will use them according to their
desert.

Ham. God's bodykins, man, much better : use every
man after his desert, and who shall 'scape whipping ?
Use them after your own honour and dignity : the less
they deserve, the more merit is in your bounty. Take
them in.

Pol. Come, sirs.

Ham. Follow him, friends : we'll hear a play to-
morrow. [*Exit Polonius with all the Players but the
First*] Dost thou hear me, old friend ; can you play
the Murder of Gonzago ?

First Play. Ay, my lord.

Ham. We'll ha't to-morrow night. You could, for
a need, study a speech of some dozen or sixteen lines,
which I would set down and insert in't, could you not ?

First Play. Ay, my lord.

Ham. Very well. Follow that lord; and look you mock him not. [*Exit First Player*] My good friends, I'll leave you till night: you are welcome to Elsinore.

Ros. Good my lord!

[*Exeunt Rosencrantz and Guildenstern.*

Ham. Ay, so, God be wi' ye:—Now I am alone.
O, what a rogue and peasant slave am I!
Is it not monstrous that this player here,
But in a fiction, in a dream of passion,
Could force his soul so to his own conceit
That from her working all his visage wann'd;
Tears in his eyes, distraction in 's aspect,
A broken voice, and his whole function suiting
With forms to his conceit? and all for nothing!
For Hecuba!
What's Hecuba to him, or he to Hecuba,
That he should weep for her?   What would he do,
Had he the motive and the cue for passion
That I have? He would drown the stage with tears
And cleave the general ear with horrid speech,
Make mad the guilty and appal the free,
Confound the ignorant, and amaze indeed
The very faculties of eyes and ears.
Yet I,
A dull and muddy-mettled rascal, peak,
Like John-a-dreams, unpregnant of my cause,
And can say nothing; no, not for a king,
Upon whose property and most dear life
A damn'd defeat was made.   Am I a coward?
Who calls me villain? breaks my pate across?
Plucks off my beard, and blows it in my face?
Tweaks me by the nose? gives me the lie i' the throat,
As deep as to the lungs? who does me this?
Ha! I should take it: for it cannot be
But I am pigeon-liver'd and lack gall
To make oppression bitter, or ere this
I should have fatted all the region kites
With this slave's offal: bloody, bloody villain!
Remorseless, treacherous, lecherous, kindless villain!

O, vengeance!
Ay sure, this is most brave,
That I, the son of a dear father murder'd,
Prompted to my revenge by heaven and hell,
Must, like a whore, unpack my heart with words
And fall a-cursing, like a very drab,
A scullion!
Fie upon't! foh! About, my brain! Hum, I have
      heard
That guilty creatures, sitting at a play,
Have by the very cunning of the scene
Been struck so to the soul, that presently
They have proclaimed their malefactions;
For murder, though it have no tongue, will speak
With most miraculous organ. I'll have these players
Play something like the murder of my father
Before mine uncle: I'll observe his looks;
I'll tent him to the quick: if he but blench,
I know my course. The spirit that I have seen
May be the devil: and the devil hath power
To assume a pleasing shape; yea, and perhaps
Out of my weakness and my melancholy,
As he is very potent with such spirits,
Abuses me to damn me: I'll have grounds
More relative than this. The play's the thing
Wherein I'll catch the conscience of the king.

ACT III.

Scene I. *The same.*

King, Queen, Polonius, Ophelia, Rosencrantz,
and Guildenstern.

King.

AND can you, by no drift of circumstance,
Get from him why he puts on this con-
fusion?

Ros. He does confess he feels himself distracted;
But from what cause he will by no means speak.

Queen. Did you assay him
To any pastime?

Ros. Madam, it so fell out, that certain players
We o'er-raught on the way: of these we told him,
And there did seem in him a kind of joy
To hear of it: they are about the court,
And, as I think, they have already order
This night to play before him.

Pol.   'Tis most true:
And he beseech'd me to entreat your majesties
To hear and see the matter.

King. With all my heart; and it doth much con-
tent me
To hear him so inclined.
Good gentlemen, give him a further edge
And drive his purpose on to these delights.
                    [*Exeunt Rosencrantz and Guildenstern.*

King. Sweet Gertrude, leave us too ;
For we have closely sent for Hamlet hither,
That he, as 'twere by accident, may here
Affront Ophelia :
Her father and myself, lawful espials,
Will so bestow ourselves that, seeing unseen,
We may of their encounter frankly judge,
And gather by him, as he is behaved,
If 't be the affliction of his love or no
That thus he suffers for.

Queen. I shall obey you.
And for your part, Ophelia, I do wish
That your good beauties be the happy cause
Of Hamlet's wildness : so shall I hope your virtues
Will bring him to his wonted way again,
To both your honours.

Oph. Madam, I wish it may. [*Exit Queen.*
Pol. Ophelia, walk you here. Gracious, so please
    you,
We will bestow ourselves. [*To Ophelia*] Read on this
    book ;
That show of such an exercise may colour
Your loneliness. [*Exit Ophelia.*
I hear him coming : let's withdraw, my lord.
[*Exeunt King and Polonius.*

Enter HAMLET.

Ham. To be, or not to be : that is the question :
Whether 'tis nobler in the mind to suffer
The slings and arrows of outrageous fortune,
Or to take arms against a sea of troubles,
And by opposing end them ?—To die ;—to sleep ;—
No more ; and by a sleep, to say we end
The heart-ache, and the thousand natural shocks
That flesh is heir to, 'tis a consummation
Devoutly to be wish'd. To die ;—to sleep ;—
To sleep ! perchance to dream :—ay, there's the rub
For in that sleep of death what dreams may come

When we have shuffled off this mortal coil,
Must give us pause.   There's the respect
That makes calamity of so long life ;
For who would bear the whips and scorns of time,
The oppressor's wrong, the proud man's contumely,
The pangs of despised love, the law's delay,
The insolence of office, and the spurns
That patient merit of the unworthy takes,
When he himself might his quietus make
With a bare bodkin ? who would these fardels bear,
To grunt and sweat under a weary life,
But that the dread of something after death,
The undiscover'd country from whose bourn
No traveller returns,—puzzles the will,
And makes us rather bear those ills we have
Than fly to others that we know not of ?
Thus conscience does make cowards of us all ;
And thus the native hue of resolution
Is sicklied o'er with the pale cast of thought,
And enterprises of great pith and moment
With this regard their currents turn awry,
And lose the name of action.   Soft you now !
The fair Ophelia !   Nymph, in thy orisons
Be all my sins remember'd.

   Oph.   Good my lord,
How does your honour for this many a day ?

   Ham. I humbly thank you ; well, well, well.

   Oph. My lord, I have remembrances of yours,
That I have longed long to re-deliver ;
I pray you, now receive them.

   Ham.   No, not I ;
I never gave you aught.

   Oph. My honour'd lord, you know right well you
      did ;
And with them words of so sweet breath composed
As made the things more rich : their perfume lost,
Take these again ; for to the noble mind
Rich gifts wax poor when givers prove unkind.
There, my lord.

Ham. Ha, ha! are you honest?

Oph. My lord?

Ham. Are you fair?

Oph. What means your lordship?

Ham. That if you be honest and fair, your honesty should admit no discourse to your beauty.

Oph. Could beauty, my lord, have better commerce than with honesty?

Ham. Ay, truly; for the power of beauty will sooner transform honesty from what it is than the force of honesty can translate beauty into his likeness: this was sometime a paradox, but now the time gives it proof. I did love you once.

Oph. Indeed, my lord, you made me believe so.

Ham. You should not have believed me; for virtue cannot so inoculate our old stock but we shall relish of it: I loved you not.

Oph. I was the more deceived.

Ham. Get thee to a nunnery: why wouldst thou be a breeder of sinners? I am myself indifferent honest; but yet I could accuse me of such things that it were better my mother had not borne me: I am very proud, revengeful, ambitious; with more offences at my beck than I have thoughts to put them in, imagination to give them shape or time to act them in. What should such fellows as I do crawling between earth and heaven? We are arrant knaves all; believe none of us. Go thy ways to a nunnery.—Where's your father?

Oph. At home, my lord.

Ham. Let the doors be shut upon him, that he may play the fool no where but in's own house. Farewell.

Oph. O, help him, you sweet heavens!

Ham. If thou dost marry, I'll give thee this plague for thy dowry: be thou as chaste as ice, as pure as snow, thou shalt not escape calumny. Get thee to a nunnery, go: farewell. Or, if thou wilt needs marry, marry a fool; for wise men know well enough what monsters you make of them. To a nunnery, go; and quickly too. Farewell.

Oph. O heavenly powers, restore him !

Ham. I have heard of your paintings too. Well enough God hath given you one face, and you make yourselves another : you jig, you amble, and you lisp, and nick-name God's creatures, and make your wantonness your ignorance. Go to, I'll no more on't ; it hath made me mad. I say, we will have no more marriages : those that are married already, all but one, shall live ; the rest shall keep as they are. To a nunnery, go.   [*Exit.*

Oph. O, what a noble mind is here o'erthrown !
The courtier's, scholar's, soldier's, eye, tongue, sword ;
The expectancy and rose of the fair state,
The glass of fashion and the mould of form,
The observed of all observers, quite, quite down !
And I, of ladies most deject and wretched,
That suck'd the honey of his music vows,
Now see that noble and most sovereign reason,
Like sweet bells jangled out of tune, and harsh ;
That unmatch'd form and feature of blown youth
Blasted with ecstacy : O, woe is me !—
To have seen what I have seen, see what I see ! [*Exit.*

Re-enter KING *and* POLONIUS.

King. Love ! his affections do not that way tend;
Nor what he spake, though it lack'd form a little,
Was not like madness. There's something in his soul,
O'er which his melancholy sits on brood ;
He shall with speed to England,
For the demand of our neglected tribute :
Haply the seas and countries different
With variable objects shall expel
This something-settled matter in his heart,
Whereon his brains still beating puts him thus
From fashion of himself. What think you on't ?

Pol. It shall do well : but yet do I believe
The origin and commencement of his grief
Sprung from neglected love.
My lord, do as you please ;
But, if you hold it fit, after the play
Let his queen mother all alone entreat him
To show his grief : let her be round with him ;
And I'll be placed, so please you, in the ear
Of all their conference. If she find him not,
To England send him, or confine him where
Your wisdom best shall think.
 King.   It shall be so.
Madness in great ones must not unwatch'd go. [*Exeunt.*

Enter HAMLET *and* Player.

Ham. Speak the speech, I pray you, as I pronounced it to you, trippingly on the tongue : but if
you mouth it, as many of your players do, I had as lief
the town-crier spoke my lines. Nor do not saw the
air too much with your hand, thus ; but use all gently ;
for in the very torrent, tempest, and, as I may say,
whirlwind of your passion, you must acquire and beget
a temperance that may give it smoothness. O, it
offends me to the soul to hear a robustious periwig-
pated fellow tear a passion to tatters, to very rags, to
split the ears of the groundlings, who for the most
part are capable of nothing but inexplicable dumb-
shows and noise : I would have such a fellow whipped
for o'erdoing Termagant ; it out-herods Herod : pray
you, avoid it.

First Play. I warrant your honour.

Ham. Be not too tame neither, but let your own
discretion be your tutor : suit the action to the word,
the word to the action ; with this special observance,
that you o'erstep not the modesty of nature ; for any
thing so overdone is from the purpose of playing,
whose end, both at the first and now, was and is, to
hold, as 'twere, the mirror up to nature ; to show virtue

her own feature, scorn her own image, and the very age and body of the time his form and pressure. Now this overdone, or come tardy off, though it make the unskilful laugh, cannot but make the judicious grieve; the censure of the which one must in your allowance o'erweigh a whole theatre of others. O, there be players that I have seen play, and heard others praise, and that highly, not to speak it profanely, that neither having the accent of Christians, nor the gait of Christian, pagan, nor man, have so strutted and bellowed, that I have thought some of nature's journeymen had made men, and not made them well, they imitated humanity so abominably.

First Play. I hope we have reformed that indifferently with us, sir.

Ham. O, reform it altogether. And let those that play your clowns speak no more than is set down for them : for there be of them that will themselves laugh, to set on some quantity of barren spectators to laugh too, though in the meantime some necessary question of the play be then to be considered : that's villanous, and shows a most pitiful ambition in the fool that uses it. Go, make you ready. [*Exeunt Players.*

Ham. Horatio!

Enter HORATIO.

Hor. Here, sweet lord, at your service.

Ham. Horatio, thou art e'en as just a man
As e'er my conversation coped withal.

Hor. O, my dear lord.

Ham.   Nay, do not think I flatter;
For what advancement may I hope from thee,
That no revenue hast but thy good spirits
To feed and clothe thee ? Why should the poor be
    flatter'd ?
No, let the candied tongue lick absurd pomp,
And crook the pregnant hinges of the knee
Where thrift may follow fawning. Dost thou hear ?

Since my dear soul was mistress of my choice
And could of men distinguish her election,
S'hath seal'd thee for herself; for thou hast been
As one, in suffering all, that suffers nothing,
A man that fortune's buffets and rewards
Hath ta'en with equal thanks: and blest are those
Whose blood and judgment are so well commingled,
That they are not a pipe for fortune's finger
To sound what stop she please. Give me that man
That is not passion's slave, and I will wear him
In my heart's core, ay, in my heart of heart,
As I do thee. Something too much of this.
There is a play to-night before the king;
One scene of it comes near the circumstance
Which I have told thee, of my father's death.
I prithee when thou seest that act afoot,
Even with the very comment of my soul
Observe my uncle: if his occulted guilt
Do not itself unkennel in one speech,
It is a damned ghost that we have seen,
And my imaginations are as foul
As Vulcan's stithy. Give him heedful note;
For I mine eyes will rivet to his face,
And after we will both our judgments join
In censure of his seeming.—
They are coming to the play; I must be idle:
Get you a place.

Danish march. Enter KING, QUEEN, POLONIUS,
OPHELIA, ROSENCRANTZ, GUILDENSTERN, *and
other Lords attendant, with the Guard carrying
torches.*

King. How fares our cousin Hamlet?
Ham. Excellent, i' faith; of the chameleon's dish:
I eat the air, promise-crammed: you cannot feed
capons so.
King. I have nothing with this answer, Hamlet;
these words are not mine.

Ham. No, nor mine now. [*To Polonius*] My lord, you played once i' the university, you say?

Pol. That did I, my lord; and was accounted a good actor.

Ham. What did you enact?

Pol. I did enact Julius Cæsar: I was killed i' the Capitol; Brutus killed me.

Ham. It was a brute part of him to kill so capital a calf there. Be the players ready?

Ros. Ay, my lord; they stay upon your patience.

Queen. Come hither, my dear Hamlet, sit by me.

Ham. No, good mother, here's metal more attractive.

Pol. [*To the King*] O, ho! do you mark that?

Ham. Lady, shall I lie in your lap?

Oph. You are merry, my lord.

Ham. O God, your only jig-maker. What should a man do but be merry? for, look you, how cheerfully my mother looks, and my father died within's two hours.

Oph. Nay, 'tis twice two months, my lord.

Ham. So long? Nay then, let the devil wear black, for I'll have a suit of sables. O heavens! die two months ago, and not forgotten yet? Then there's hope a great man's memory may outlive his life half a year: but, by'r lady, he must build churches then.

Oph. What means this play, my lord?

Ham. Miching mallecho; it means mischief.

Oph. But what is the argument of the play.

Enter Prologue.

Ham. We shall know by this fellow.

Prologue. '*For us and for our tragedy,*
    '*Here stooping to your clemency,*
    '*We beg your hearing patiently.*' [*Exit.*

Ham. Is this a prologue, or the posy of a ring?

Oph. 'Tis brief, my lord.
Ham. As woman's love.

Enter two Players *as* King *and* Queen.

P. King. ' Full thirty times hath Phœbus' cart gone
    round
' Neptune's salt wash and Tellus' orbed ground,
' Since love our hearts and Hymen did our hands
' Unite commutual in most sacred bands.
    P. Queen. 'So many journeys may the sun and moon
' Make us again count o'er ere love be done !
' But, woe is me, you are so sick of late,
' So far from cheer and from your former state,
' That I distrust you.   Yet, though I distrust,
' Discomfort you, my lord, it nothing must.
    P. King. ' Faith, I must leave thee, love, and shortly
    too ;
' My operant powers their functions leave to do :
' And thou shalt live in this fair world behind,
' Honour'd, beloved ; and haply one as kind
' For husband shalt thou—
    P. Queen.   ' O, confound the rest !
' Such love must needs be treason in my breast :
' In second husband let me be accurst !
' None wed the second but who kill'd the first.
    Ham. [*Aside*] Wormwood, wormwood.
    P. King. ' I do believe you think what now you
    speak ;
' But what we do determine oft we break.
' What to ourselves in passion we propose,
' The passion ending, doth the purpose lose.
' So think thou wilt no second husband wed ;
' But die thy thoughts when thy first lord is dead.
    P. Queen. ' Nor earth to me give food, nor heaven
    light !
' Sport and repose lock from me day and night !
' Both here and hence pursue me lasting strife,
' If, once a widow, ever I be wife !

P. King. ' 'Tis deeply sworn.

Ham. If she should break it now!

P. King. ' Sweet, leave me here awhile ;

' My spirits grow dull, and fain I would beguile

' The tedious day with sleep.   [*Sleeps.*

    P. Queen.   ' Sleep rock thy brain !

' And never come mischance between us twain ! [*Exit.*

Ham. Madam, how like you this play ?

Queen. The lady doth protest too much, methinks.

Ham. O, but she'll keep her word.

King. Have you heard the argument ? Is there no offence in't ?

Ham. No, no, they do but jest, poison in jest; no offence i' the world.

King. What do you call the play ?

Ham. The Mouse-trap. Marry, how ? Tropically. This play is the image of a murder done in Vienna ; Gonzago is the duke's name ; his wife, Baptista : you shall see anon ; 'tis a knavish piece of work : but what o' that ? your majesty and we that have free souls, it touches us not : let the galled jade wince, our withers are unwrung.

Enter Player *as* Lucianus.

This is one Lucianus, nephew to the king.

Oph. You are as good as a chorus, my lord.

Ham. I could interpret between you and your love, if I could see the puppets dallying.

Begin, murderer ; leave thy damnable faces, and begin. Come : "the croaking raven doth bellow for revenge."

Luc. 'Thoughts black, hands apt, drugs fit, and time agreeing ;

' Confederate season, else no creature seeing ;

' Thou mixture rank, of midnight weeds collected,

' With Hecate's ban thrice blasted, thrice infected,

' Thy natural magic and dire property,

' On wholesome life usurp immediately.'

       [*Pours the poison into the sleeper's ear.*

E

Ham. He poisons him i' the garden for his estate. His name's Gonzago: the story is extant, and written in very choice Italian: you shall see anon how the murderer gets the love of Gonzago's wife.

King. Give me some light : away !

All. Lights, lights, lights !

Ham. What, frighted with false fire ?

> [*Exeunt all but Hamlet and Horatio.*

> For thou dost know, O Damon dear,
>   This realm dismantled was
> Of Jove himself ; and now reigns here
>   A very, very—peacock.

Hor. You might have rhymed.

Ham. O good Horatio, I'll take the ghost's word for a thousand pound.   Didst perceive ?

Hor. Very well, my lord.

Ham. Upon the talk of the poisoning ?

Hor. I did very well note him.

Ham. Ah, ha ! Come, some music ! come, the re-corders !

> For if the king like not the comedy,
> Why then, belike, he likes it not, perdy.

Come, some music.

Re-enter ROSENCRANTZ *and* GUILDENSTERN.

Guil. Good my lord, vouchsafe me a word with you.

Ham. Sir, a whole history.

Guil. The king, sir,—

Ham. Ay, sir, what of him ?

Guil. Is in his retirement marvellous distempered.

Ham. With drink, sir ?

Guil. No, my lord, with choler.

Ham. Your wisdom should show itself more richer to signify this to the doctor : for, for me to put him to his purgation would perhaps plunge him into far more choler.

Guil. Good my lord, put your discourse into some frame and start not so wildly from my affair.

Ham. I am tame, sir : pronounce.

Guil. The queen, your mother, in most great affliction of spirit, hath sent me to you.

Ham.· You are welcome.

Guil. Nay, good my lord, this courtesy is not of the
right breed. If it shall please you to make me a
wholesome answer, I will do your mother's commandment : if not, your pardon and my return shall be the
end of my business.

Ham. Sir, I cannot.

Guil. What, my lord ?

Ham. Make you a wholesome answer; my wit's
diseased : but, sir, such answer as I can make, you shall
command ; or rather, as you say, my mother : therefore no more, but to the matter : my mother, you say,—

Ros. Then thus she says; your behaviour hath
struck her into amazement and admiration.

Ham. O wonderful son, that can so astonish a
mother ! But is there no sequel at the heels of this
mother's admiration ?   Impart.

Ros. She desires to speak with you in her closet, ere
you go to bed.

Ham. We shall obey, were she ten times our mother.
Have you any further trade with us?

Ros. My lord, you once did love me.

Ham. So I do still, by these pickers and stealers.

Ros. Good my lord, what is your cause of distemper ?
you do surely bar the door upon your own liberty, if
you deny your griefs to your friend.

Ham. Sir, I lack advancement.

Ros. How can that be, when you have the voice
of the king himself for your succession in Denmark ?

Ham. Ay, sir, but "While the grass grows,"—the
proverb is something musty.

Re-enter HORATIO *and* Players *with* Recorders.

O, the recorders ! let me see one. To withdraw with

you :—why do you go about to recover the wind of me, as if you would drive me into a toil ?

Guil. O, my lord, if my duty be too bold, my love is too unmannerly.

Ham. I do not well understand that. Will you play upon this pipe?

Guil. My lord, I cannot.

Ham. I pray you.

Guil. Believe me, I cannot.

Ham. I do beseech you.

Ros. I know no touch of it, my lord.

Ham. 'Tis as easy as lying : govern these ventages with your fingers and thumb, give it breath with your mouth, and it will discourse most eloquent music. Look you, these are the stops.

Guil. But these cannot I command to any utterance of harmony ; I have not the skill.

Ham. Why, look you now, how unworthy a thing you make of me ! You would play upon me ; you would seem to know my stops ; you would pluck out the heart of my mystery ; you would sound me from my lowest note to the top of my compass : and there is much music, excellent voice, in this little organ ; yet cannot you make it speak. 'Sblood, do you think I am easier to be played on than a pipe ? Call me what instrument you will, though you can fret me, yet you cannot play upon me. Besides, to be demanded of a sponge !

Ros. Take you me for a sponge, my lord?

Ham. Ay, sir, that soaks up the king's countenance, his rewards, his authorities. But such officers do the king best service in the end : he keeps them, as an ape doth nuts, in the corner of his jaw ; first mouthed, to be last swallowed : when he needs what you have gleaned, it is but squeezing you, and, sponge, you shall be dry again—you shall !

Ros. I understand you not, my lord.

Ham. I am glad of it : a knavish speech sleeps in a foolish ear.

Enter POLONIUS.

God bless you, sir !

Pol. My lord, the queen would speak with you, and presently.

Ham. Do you see yonder cloud that's almost in shape of a camel ?

Pol. By the mass, and 'tis like a camel, indeed.

Ham. Methinks it is like a weasel.

Pol. It is backed like a weasel.

Ham. Or like a whale ?

Pol. Very like a whale.

Ham. Then I will come to my mother by and by. [*Aside*] They fool me to the top of my bent.—I will come by and by.

Pol. I will say so.   [*Exit Polonius.*

Ham. " By and by " is easily said.   Leave me, friends.   [*Exeunt Rosencrantz and Guildenstern.*

Ham. Good night, Horatio.

Hor. Good night unto your lordship. [*Exit Horatio.*

Ham. 'Tis now the very witching time of night,
When churchyards yawn and hell itself breathes out
Contagion to this world : now could I drink hot blood,
And do such bitter business as the day
Would quake to look on.   Soft ! now to my mother.
O heart, lose not thy nature ; let not ever
The soul of Nero enter this firm bosom :
Let me be cruel, not unnatural :
I will speak daggers to her, but use none.   [*Exit.*

SCENE II.   *A room in the castle.*

Enter KING, ROSENCRANTZ, *and* GUILDENSTERN.

King.

 LIKE him not, nor stands it safe with us
      To let his madness range.   Therefore prepare
           you ;
I your commission will forthwith dispatch,
And he to England shall along with you :
Arm you, I pray you, to this speedy voyage ;
For we will fetters put upon this fear,
Which now goes too free-footed.

   Ros. ⎱   We will haste us.
   Guil. ⎰

        [*Exeunt Rosencrantz and Guildenstern.*
   King. O, my offence is rank, it smells to heaven ;
It hath the primal eldest curse upon't,
A brother's murder.   Pray can I not,
Though inclination be as sharp as will :
My stronger guilt defeats my strong intent ;
And, like a man to double business bound,
I stand in pause where I shall first begin,
And both neglect.   What if this cursed hand
Were thicker than itself with brother's blood,
Is there not rain enough in the sweet heavens
To wash it white as snow ?   Whereto serves mercy
But to confront the visage of offence ?
And what's in prayer but this twofold force,
To be forestalled ere we come to fall,
Or pardon'd being down ?   Then I'll look up ;
My fault is past.   But O, what form of prayer
Can serve my turn ?   " Forgive me my foul murder ?"
That cannot be ; since I am still possess'd
Of those effects for which I did the murder,
My crown, mine own ambition and my queen.

May one be pardon'd and retain the offence?
In the corrupted currents of this world
Offence's gilded hand may shove by justice,
And oft 'tis seen the wicked prize itself
Buys out the law: but 'tis not so above;
There is no shuffling, there the action lies
In his true nature, and we ourselves compell'd,
·Even to the teeth and forehead of our faults,
To give in evidence. What then? what rests?
Try what repentance can: what can it not?
Yet what can it when one can not repent?
O wretched state! O bosom black as death!
O limed soul, that struggling to be free
Art more engaged! Help, angels! make assay!
                                        [*Kneels.*
Bow, stubborn knees; and, heart with strings of steel,
Be soft as sinews of the new-born babe!
All may be well.
[*Rising*] My words fly up, my thoughts remain
        below:
Words without thoughts never to heaven go. [*Exit.*

SCENE III. *Another room in the same.*

Enter QUEEN *and* POLONIUS.

Polonius.

E will come straight. Look you lay home to
        him:
Tell him his pranks have been too broad to
    bear with,
And that your grace hath screen'd and stood between
Much heat and him. I'll sconce me even here.
Pray you, be round with him.
    Queen. I'll warrant you, fear me not. Withdraw, I
        hear him coming.
                    [*Polonius hides behind the arras.*

Enter HAMLET.

Ham. Now, mother, what's the matter?

Queen. Hamlet, thou hast thy father much offended.

Ham. Mother, you have my father much offended.

Queen. Come, come, you answer with an idle tongue.

Ham. Go, go, you question with a wicked tongue.

Queen. Why, how now, Hamlet!

Ham. What's the matter now?

Queen. Have you forgot me?

Ham. No, by the rood, not so:
You are the queen, your husband's brother's wife;
And—would it were not so!—you are my mother.

Queen. Nay, then, I'll set those to you that can speak.

Ham. Come, come, and sit you down; you shall not
    budge;
You go not till I set you up a glass
Where you may see the inmost part of you.

Queen. What wilt thou do? thou wilt not murder
    me? Help, help, ho!

Pol. [*Behind*] What, ho! help, help, help!

Ham. [*Drawing*] How now! a rat? Dead, for a
    ducat, dead! [*Makes a pass through the arras.*

Pol. [*Behind*] O, I am slain! [*Falls and dies.*

Queen. O me, what hast thou done?

Ham. Nay, I know not: is it the king?

Queen. O, what a rash and bloody deed is this!

Ham. A bloody deed! almost as bad, good mother,
As kill a king, and marry with his brother.

Queen. As kill a king!

Ham. Ay, lady, 'twas my word.
    [*Lifts up the arras and discovers Polonius.*
Thou wretched, rash, intruding fool, farewell!
I took thee for thy better:
Leave wringing of your hands: peace! sit you down,
And let me wring your heart; for so I shall,
If it be made of penetrable stuff,
If damned custom have not brass'd it so
That it be proof and bulwark against sense.

Queen. What have I done, that thou darest wag thy
    tongue
In noise so rude against me?
    Ham.   Such an act
That blurs the grace and blush of modesty,
Calls virtue hypocrite, takes off the rose
From the fair forehead of an innocent love
And sets a blister there, makes marriage-vows
As false as dicers' oaths : O, such a deed
As from the body of contraction plucks
The very soul, and sweet religion makes
A rhapsody of words : heaven's face doth glow ;
Yea, this solidity and compound mass,
With tristful visage, as against the doom,
Is thought-sick at the act.
    Queen. Ah me, what act ?
    Ham. Look here, upon this picture, and on this,
The counterfeit presentment of two brothers.
See, what a grace was seated on his brow ;
Hyperion's curls, the front of Jove himself,
An eye like Mars, to threaten and command ;
A station like the herald Mercury
New-lighted on a heaven-kissing hill ;
A combination and a form indeed,
Where every god did seem to set his seal
To give the world assurance of a man :
This was your husband.   Look you now, what follows :
Here is your husband ; like a mildew'd ear,
Blasting his wholesome brother.   Have you eyes ?
Could you on this fair mountain leave to feed,
And batten on this moor ?   Ha ! have you eyes ?
You cannot call it love, for at your age
The hey-day in the blood is tame, it's humble,
And waits upon the judgment : and what judgment
Would step from this to this ?
O shame ! where is thy blush ?   Rebellious hell,
If thou canst mutine in a matron's bones,
To flaming youth let virtue be as wax,
And melt in her own fire : proclaim no shame

When the compulsive ardour gives the charge,
Since frost itself as actively doth burn
And reason panders will.

   Queen.   O Hamlet, speak no more :
Thou turn'st mine eyes into my very soul.

   Ham.   Nay, but to live
In the rank sweat of an incestuous bed.

   Queen. No more, sweet Hamlet !

   Ham.   A murderer and a villain ;
A slave that is not twentieth part the tithe
Of your precedent lord ; a vice of kings ;
A cutpurse of the empire and the rule,
That from a shelf the precious diadem stole,
And put it in his pocket !

   Queen.   No more !

   Ham. A king of shreds and patches—

Enter Ghost.

Save me, and hover o'er me with your wings,
You heavenly guards ! What would you, gracious
      figure ?

   Queen. Alas, he's mad !

   Ham. Do you not come your tardy son to chide,
That, lapsed in time and passion, lets go by
The important acting of your dread command ?
O, say !

   Ghost. Do not forget : this visitation
Is but to whet thy almost blunted purpose.
But look, amazement on thy mother sits :
O, step between her and her fighting soul :
Speak to her, Hamlet.

   Ham.   How is it with you, lady ?

   Queen. Alas, how is't with you,
That you do bend your eye on vacancy
And with the incorporal air do hold discourse ?
Forth at your eyes your spirits wildly peep ;
O gentle son,
Upon the heat and flame of thy distemper

Sprinkle cool patience.   Whereon do you look?

   Ham. On him, on him! Look you, how pale he
       glares!

His form and cause conjoin'd, preaching to stones·

Would make them capable.   Do not look upon me;

Lest with this piteous action you convert

My stern effects: then what I have to do

Will want true colour; tears perchance for blood.

   Queen. To whom do you speak this?

   Ham.   Do you see nothing there?

   Queen. Nothing at all; yet all that is I see.

   Ham. Nor did you nothing hear?

   Queen.   No, nothing but ourselves.

   Ham. Why, look you there! look, how it steals
       away!

My father, in his habit as he lived!

Look, where he goes, even now, out at the portal!

                          [*Exit Ghost.*

   Queen. This is the very coinage of your brain:

This bodiless creation ecstasy

Is very cunning in.

   Ham.   Ecstasy!

My pulse, as yours, doth temperately keep time,

And makes as healthful music: it is not madness

That I have utter'd: bring me to the test,

And I the matter will re-word; which madness

Would gambol from.   Mother, for love of grace,

Lay not that flattering unction to your soul,

That not your trespass but my madness speaks:

It will but skin and film the ulcerous place,

Whiles rank corruption, mining all within,

Infects unseen.   Confess yourself to Heaven;

Repent what's past, avoid what is to come.

   Queen. O Hamlet, thou hast cleft my heart in twain.

   Ham. O, throw away the worser part of it,

And live the purer with the other half.

Good night: but go not to my uncle's bed;

Assume a virtue, if you have it not.

Once more, good night:

And when you are desirous to be blest,
I'll blessing beg of you.   So again, good night!
For this same lord,   [*Pointing to Polonius.*
I do repent: but Heaven hath pleased it so,
To punish me with this and this with me,
That I must be their scourge and minister.
Good night, mother.   [*Exit Queen.*
I must be cruel, only to be kind:
Thus bad begins, and worse remains behind.
                                 [*Goes to arras.*

ACT IV.

SCENE I. *A room of state in the palace.*

Enter QUEEN *and* MARCELLUS.

Queen.

 WILL not speak with her.
    Mar. She is importunate, indeed dis-
        tract :
'Twere good she were spoken with; for
she may strew
Dangerous conjectures in ill-breeding minds.
    Queen. Let her come in.   *[Exit Marcellus.*
[Aside] To my sick soul, as sin's true nature is,
Each toy seems prologue to some great amiss.

Re-enter MARCELLUS *with* OPHELIA.

Oph. Where is the beauteous majesty of Denmark ?
Queen. How now, Ophelia !
Oph. *[Sings] How should I your true love know*
           From another one ?
       By his cockle hat and staff,
        And his sandal shoon.
Queen. Alas, sweet lady, what imports this song ?
Oph. Say you ? nay, pray you, mark.
    [Sings] He is dead and gone, lady,
        He is dead and gone ;
      At his head a grass-green turf,
       At his heels a stone.

Oh, oh !

Queen. Nay, but, Ophelia,—
Oph.   Pray you, mark.
  [*Sings*] *White his shroud as the mountain snow,—*

Enter KING.

Queen. Alas, look here, my lord.
Oph. [*Sings*] *Larded with sweet flowers ;*
              Which bewept to the grave did go
              With true-love showers.
King. How do you, pretty lady ?
Oph. Well, God 'ild you! They say the owl was a
baker's daughter. Lord, we know what we are, but
know not what we may be. God be at your table.
King. Conceit upon her father.
Oph. Pray you, let's have no words of this ; but
when they ask you what it means, say you this :
  [*Sings*] *To-morrow is Saint Valentine's day,*
              All in the morning betime,
              And I a maid at your window,
              To be your Valentine.
King. How long hath she been thus ?
Oph. I hope all will be well. We must be patient :
but I cannot choose but weep, to think they should lay
him i' the cold ground. My brother shall know of it :
and so I thank you for your good counsel. Come, my
coach! Good night, ladies ; good night, sweet ladies ;
good night, good night.   [*Exit.*
King. Follow her close ; give her good watch, I pray
          you.   [*Exit Marcellus.*
O, this is the poison of deep grief ; it springs
All from her father's death. O Gertrude, Gertrude,
When sorrows come, they come not single spies,
But in battalions.   [*A noise within.*
  Queen.   Alack, what noise is this ?

Enter MARCELLUS.

King. What is the matter ?
Mar.   Save yourself, my lord :

The young Laertes, in a riotous head,
O'erbears your officers. The rabble call him lord:
They cry "Choose we: Laertes shall be king!"
Caps, hands and tongues applaud it to the clouds:
"Laertes shall be king, Laertes king!" [*Noise within.*

Enter LAERTES, *armed;* Danes *following.*

Laer. Where is this king? Sirs, stand you all with-
 out.
I pray you, give me leave.
 Danes.   We will, we will.
        [*They retire without the door.*
 Laer. O thou vile king,
Give me my father!
 Queen.   Calmly, good Laertes.
 King. What is the cause, Laertes,
That thy rebellion looks so giant-like?
Let him go, Gertrude; do not fear our person:
There's such divinity doth hedge a king,
That treason can but peep to what it would,
Acts little of his will. Tell me, Laertes,
Why thou art incensed. Let him go, Gertrude.
 Laer. Where is my father?
 King.   Dead.
 Queen.   But not by him.
 King. Let him demand his fill.
 Laer. How came he dead? I'll not be juggled with:
To hell, allegiance! To this point I stand,
That both the worlds I give to negligence,
Let come what comes; only I'll be revenged
Most throughly for my father.
 King.   Who shall stay you?
 Laer. My will, not all the world:
And for my means, I'll husband them so well,
They shall go far with little.
 King.   Good Laertes,
That I am guiltless of your father's death,
And am most sensibly in grief for it,

It shall as level to your judgment pierce
As day does to your eye.

    Laer. What noise is that?

Re-enter OPHELIA.

O rose of May!
Dear maid, kind sister, sweet Ophelia!
O heavens, is 't possible, a young maid's wits
Should be as mortal as an old man's life?

    Oph. [*Sings*] *They bore him bare-faced on the bier;*
        Hey non nonny, nonny, hey nonny;
        And in his grave rains many a tear,—

Fare you well, my dove!

    Laer. Had'st thou thy wits, and didst persuade re-
        venge,

It could not move thus.

    Oph. [*Sings*] *You must sing a-down, a-down,*
        An you call him a-down-a.

Oh, how the wheel becomes it. It is the false steward,
that stole his master's daughter.

    Laer. This nothing 's more than matter.

    Oph. There's rosemary, that's for remembrance;
pray, love, remember: and there is pansies, that's for
thoughts.

    Laer. A document in madness, thoughts and re-
membrance fitted.

    Oph. There's fennel for you, and columbines: there's
rue for you; and here's some for me: we may call it
herb of grace o' Sundays: O, you must wear your rue
with a difference. There's a daisy: I would give you
some violets, but they withered all when my father
died: they say he made a good end,—

    [*Sings*] *For bonny sweet Robin is all my joy.*

    Laer. Thought and affliction, passion, hell itself,
She turns to favour and to prettiness.

    Oph. [*Sings*] *And will a' not come again?*
        And will a' not come again?

> *No, no, he is dead:*
> *Go to thy death-bed:*
> *He never will come again.*
>
> *His beard was as white as snow,*
> *All flaxen was his poll:*
> *He is gone, he is gone,*
> *And we cast away moan:*
> *God ha' mercy on his soul!*

And of all Christian souls, I pray God. God be wi'
you. [*Exit Ophelia, followed by Queen and Marcellus.*
    King. Laertes, I must commune with your grief,
Or you deny me right. Go but apart,
Make choice of whom your wisest friends you will,
And they shall hear and judge 'twixt you and me:
If by direct or by collateral hand
They find us touch'd, we will our kingdom give,
Our crown, our life, and all that we call ours,
To you in satisfaction.

Enter a Messenger.

How now! what news?
    Messenger.   Letters, my lord, from Hamlet:
This to your majesty: this to the queen.
    King.   Laertes, you shall hear them.
Leave us.   [*Exit Messenger.*
    [*Reads*] "High and mighty, You shall know I am
set naked on your kingdom. To-morrow shall I beg
leave to see your kingly eyes: when I shall, first ask-
ing your pardon thereunto, recount the occasion of my
sudden and more strange return.

                     "HAMLET."

What should this mean? Are all the rest come back?
Or is it some abuse, and no such thing?
    Laer. Know you the hand?
    King.   'Tis Hamlet's character. "Naked!"
And in a postscript here, he says "alone."
Can you advise me?

Laer. I'm lost in it, my lord.   But let him come ;
It warms the very sickness in my heart,
That I shall live and tell him to his teeth,
" Thus didest thou."
   King.   If it be so, Laertes—
Will you be ruled by me ?
   Laer.   Ay, my lord ;
So you will not o'errule me to a peace.
   King. To thine own peace.
You have been talked of since your travel much,
And that in Hamlet's hearing, for a quality
Wherein, they say, you shine.
   Laer. What part is that, my lord ?
   King. A very riband in the cap of youth.
Here was a gentleman of Normandy,—
He made confession of you,
And gave you such a masterly report
For art and exercise in your defence
And for your rapier most especial,
That he cried out, 'twould be a sight indeed
If one could match you.   Sir, this report of his
Did Hamlet so envenom with his envy
That he could nothing do but wish and beg
Your sudden coming o'er, to play with him.
Now, out of this—
   Laer.   What out of this, my lord ?
   King. Hamlet return'd shall know you are come
      home :
We'll put on those shall praise your excellence
And set a double varnish on the fame
The Frenchman gave you, bring you in fine together,
And wager on your heads : he, being remiss,
Most generous and free from all contriving,
Will not peruse the foils ; so that with ease,
Or with a little shuffling, you may choose
A sword unbated, and in a pass of practice
Requite him for your father.
   Laer.   I will do't
And for that purpose I'll anoint my sword,

That, if I gall him slightly,
It may be death.
   King.   Let's further think of this.
We'll make a solemn wager on your cunnings:
I ha't:
When in your motion you are hot and dry—
As make your bouts more violent to that end—
And that he calls for drink, I'll have prepared him
A chalice for the nonce, whereon but sipping,
If he by chance escape your venom'd stuck,
Our purpose may hold there.

Enter QUEEN.

   Queen. One woe doth tread upon another's heel,
So fast they follow : your sister's drown'd, Laertes.
   Laer. Drown'd ! O, where ?
   Queen. There is a willow grows aslant a brook,
That shows his hoar leaves in the glassy stream ;
There with fantastic garlands did she come
Of crow-flowers, nettles, daisies, and long purples ;
There, on the pendent boughs her coronet weeds
Clambering to hang, an envious sliver broke ;
When down her weedy trophies and herself
Fell in the weeping brook.
   Laer. I forbid my tears : but yet
It is our trick ; nature her custom holds,
Let shame say what it will. Adieu, my lord :
I have a speech of fire, that fain would blaze,
But that this folly drowns it.   *[Exit Laertes.*

ACT V.

Scene I. *A Church Yard.*

Enter two Clowns, *with spades, &c.*

First Clown.

S she to be buried in Christian burial that wilfully seeks her own salvation?

Second· Clo. I tell thee she is; and therefore make her grave straight: the crowner hath sat on her, and finds it Christian burial.

First Clo. How can that be, unless she drowned herself in her own defence?

Second Clo. Why, 'tis found so.

First Clo. It must be "se offendendo;" it cannot be else. For here lies the point: if I drown myself wittingly, it argues an act: and an act hath three branches; it is, to act, to do, and to perform : argal, she drowned herself wittingly.

Second Clo. Nay, but hear you, goodman delver.

First Clo. Give me leave. Here lies the water; good: here stands the man; good: if the man go to this water and drown himself, it is, will he, nill he, he goes; mark you that; but if the water come to him and drown him, he drowns not himself: argal, he that is not guilty of his own death shortens not his own life.

Second Clo. But is this law?

First Clo. Ay, marry, is't; crowner's quest law.

Second Clo. Will you ha' the truth on't? If this had not been a gentlewoman, she should have been buried out o' Christian burial.

First Clo. Why, there thou say'st: and the more pity that great folk should have countenance in this world to drown or hang themselves, more than their even Christian. Come, my spade. There is no ancient gentlemen but gardeners, ditchers and grave-makers: they hold up Adam's profession.

Second Clo. Was he a gentleman?

First Clo. A' was the first that ever bore arms. I'll put a question to thee: if thou answerest me not to the purpose, confess thyself—

Second Clo. Go to.

First Clo. What is he that builds stronger than either the mason, the shipwright, or the carpenter?

Second Clo. The gallows-maker; for that frame outlives a thousand tenants.

First Clo. I like thy wit well, in good faith: the gallows does well; but how does it well? it does well to those that do ill: now thou dost ill to say the gallows is built stronger than the church: argal, the gallows may do well to thee. To't again, come.

Second Clo. Who builds stronger than a mason, a shipwright, or a carpenter?

First Clo. Ay, tell me that, and unyoke.

Second Clo. Marry, now I can tell.

First Clo. To 't.

Second Clo. Mass, I cannot tell.

First Clo. Cudgel thy brains no more about it, for your dull ass will not mend his pace with beating; and, when you are asked this question next, say "a grave-maker:" the houses that he makes last till doomsday. Go, get thee to Yaughan: fetch me a stoup of liquor.   [*Exit Second Clown.*

Enter HAMLET *and* HORATIO, *afar off.*

[*Clown digs and sings*]
   In youth, when I did love, did love,
     Methought it was very sweet,
   To contract, O, the time, for-a my behove,
     O, methought, there-a was nothing-a meet.

Ham. Has this fellow no feeling of his business, that he sings at grave-making?

Hor. Custom hath made it in him a property of easiness.

Ham. 'Tis e'en so: the hand of little employment hath the daintier sense.

First Clo. [*Sings*]
> *But age, with his stealing steps,*
> *Hath claw'd me in his clutch,*
> *And hath shipped me into the land,*
> *As if I had never been such.*

> [*Throws up a skull.*

Ham. That skull had a tongue in it, and could sing once: how the knave jowls it to the ground, as if it were Cain's jawbone, that did the first murder! It might be the pate of a politician, which this ass now o'er-reaches; one that would circumvent God, might it not?

Hor. It might, my lord.

Ham. Did these bones cost no more the breeding, but to play at loggats with 'em? mine ache to think on 't.

First Clo. [*Sings*]
> *A pick-axe, and a spade, a spade,*
> *For—and a shrouding sheet:*
> *O, a pit of clay for to be made*
> *For such a guest is meet.*

> [*Throws up another skull.*

Ham. There's another: why may not that be the skull of a lawyer? Where be his quiddities now, his quillets, his cases, his tenures, and his tricks? why does he suffer this rude knave now to knock him about the sconce with a dirty shovel, and will not tell him of his action of battery?—I will speak to this fellow. Whose grave's this, sirrah?

First Clo. Mine, sir.

> [*Sings*] *O, a pit of clay for to be made*
> *For such a guest is meet.*

Ham. I think it be thine, indeed: for thou liest in 't.

First Clo. You lie out on't sir, and therefore 'tis not yours: for my part, I do not lie in 't, and yet it is mine.

Ham. Thou dost lie in 't, to be in 't and say it is thine: 'tis for the dead, not for the quick; therefore thou liest.

First Clo. 'Tis a quick lie, sir; 'twill away again, from me to you.

Ham. What man dost thou dig it for?

First Clo. For no man, sir.

Ham. What woman, then?

First Clo. For none, neither.

Ham. Who is to buried in 't?

First Clo. One that was a woman, sir; but, rest her soul, she's dead.

Ham. How absolute the knave is! we must speak by the card, or equivocation will undo us. How long hast thou been a grave-maker?

First Clo. Of all the days i' the year, I came to 't that day that our last king Hamlet overcame Fortinbras.

Ham. How long is that since?

First Clo. Cannot you tell that? every fool can tell that: it was the very day that young Hamlet was born: he that is mad, and sent into England.

Ham. Ay, marry, why was he sent into England?

First Clo. Why, because a' was mad: a' shall recover his wits there; or, if a' do not, it 's no great matter there.

Ham. Why?

First Clo. 'Twill not be seen in him there; there the men are as mad as he.

Ham. How came he mad?

First Clo. Very strangely, they say.

Ham. How "strangely?"

First Clo. Faith, e'en with losing his wits.

Ham. Upon what ground?

First Clo. Why, here in Denmark: I have been sexton here, man and boy, thirty years.

Ham. How long will a man lie i' the earth ere he rot?

First Clo. I' faith, if a' be not rotten before a' die, a' will last you some eight year or nine year: a tanner will last you nine year.

Ham. Why he more than another?

First Clo. Why, sir, his hide is so tanned with his trade, that a' will keep out water a great while; and your water is a sore decayer of your dead body. Here's a skull now; this skull hath lain in the earth three and twenty years.

Ham. Whose was it?

First Clo. A mad fellow's it was: whose do you think it was?

Ham. Nay, I know not.

First Clo. A pestilence on him for a mad rogue! a' poured a flagon of Rhenish on my head once. This same skull, sir, was Yorick's skull, the king's jester.

Ham. This?

First Clo. E'en that.

Ham. [*Takes the skull*] Alas, poor Yorick! I knew him, Horatio: a fellow of infinite jest, of most excellent fancy: he hath borne me on his back a thousand times. Here hung those lips that I have kissed I know not how oft. Where be your gibes now? your gambols? your songs? your flashes of merriment, that were wont to set the table on a roar? Not one now to mock your own grinning? quite chop-fallen? Now get you to my lady's chamber, and tell her, let her paint an inch thick, to this favour she must come; make her laugh at that. Prithee, Horatio, tell me one thing.

Hor. What's that, my lord?

Ham. Dost thou think Alexander looked o' this fashion i' the earth?

Hor. E'en so.

Ham. And smelt so? pah! [*Puts down the skull.*

Hor. E'en so, my lord.

Ham. To what base uses we may return, Horatio!

Why may not imagination trace the noble dust of
Alexander, till he find it stopping a bung-hole?

Hor. 'Twere to consider too curiously, to consider
so.

Ham. No, faith, not a jot; but to follow him thither
with modesty enough, and likelihood to lead it: as
thus: Alexander died, Alexander was buried, Alexander returneth into dust; the dust is earth; of earth
we make loam; and why of that loam, whereto he was
converted, might they not stop a beer-barrel?

Imperious Cæsar dead and turn'd to clay,
Might stop a hole to keep the wind away:
O, that that earth, which kept the world in awe,
Should patch a wall to expel the winter's flaw!
But soft! but soft! aside: here comes the king,
The queen, the courtiers: who is this they follow?
And with such maimed rites? This doth betoken
The corse they follow did with desperate hand
Fordo its own life: 'twas of some estate.
Couch we awhile, and mark. [*Retiring with Horatio.*

Enter Priests, &c. *in procession; the Corpse of Ophelia,*
LAERTES *and* Mourners *following;* KING, QUEEN,
their trains, &c.

Laertes. What ceremony else?
Ham. That is Laertes, a very noble youth.
Laertes. What ceremony else?
Priest. Her obsequies have been as far enlarged
As we have warranty: her death was doubtful;
And, but that great command o'ersways the order,
She should in ground unsanctified have lodged
Till the last trumpet; for charitable prayers,
Shards, flints and pebbles should be thrown on her:
Yet here she is allow'd her virgin crants,
Her maiden strewments and the bringing home
Of bell and burial.
Laer. Must there no more be done?
First Priest.   No more be done:
We should profane the service of the dead

To sing a requiem and such rest to her
As to peace-parted souls.

  Laer.   Lay her i' the earth:
And from her fair and unpolluted flesh
May violets spring! I tell thee churlish priest,
A ministering angel shall my sister be,
When thou liest howling.

  Ham.   What, the fair Ophelia!

  Queen. Sweets to the sweet: farewell!

             [Scattering flowers.
I hoped thou shouldst have been my Hamlet's wife;
I thought thy bride-bed to have deck'd, sweet maid,
And not have strew'd thy grave.

  Laer.   O, treble woe
Fall ten times treble on that cursed head,
Whose wicked deed thy most ingenious sense
Deprived thee of! Hold off the earth awhile,
Till I have caught her once more in mine arms:

         [Leaps into the grave.
Now pile your dust upon the quick and dead,
Till of this flat a mountain you have made,
To o'ertop old Pelion, or the skyish head
Of blue Olympus.

  Ham. [*Advancing*] What is he whose grief
Bears such an emphasis? whose phrase of sorrow
Conjures the wandering stars, and makes them stand
Like wonder-wounded hearers? This is I,
Hamlet the Dane.

  Laer.   The devil take thy soul!

          [Grappling with him.

  Ham. Thou pray'st not well.
I prithee, take thy fingers from my throat;
For, though I am not splenitive and rash,
Yet have I something in me dangerous,
Which let thy wisdom fear: hold off thy hand.

  King. Pluck them asunder.

  Queen. Hamlet, Hamlet!

  All. Gentlemen!

  Hor. Good, my lord—

Ham. Why, I will fight with him upon this theme
Until my eyelids will no longer wag.
  Queen. O my son, what theme?
  Ham. I loved Ophelia : forty thousand brothers
Could not, with all their quantity of love,
Make up my sum.   What wilt thou do for her?
  King. O, he is mad, Laertes.
  Ham. 'Swounds, show me what thou'lt do :
Woo't weep? woo't fight? woo't fast? woo't tear thy-
      self?
I'll do't! I'll do't!   Dost thou come here to whine?
To outface me with leaping in her grave?
Be buried quick with her, and so will I :
And, if thou prate of mountains, let them throw
Millions of acres on us, till our ground,
Singeing its pate against the burning zone,
Make Ossa like a wart!   Nay, an thou'lt mouth,
I'll rant as well as thou.
  Queen.   This is mere madness :
And thus awhile the fit will work on him ;
Anon, as patient as the female dove,
When that her golden couplets are disclosed,
His silence will sit drooping.
  Ham.   Hear you, sir ;
What is the reason that you use me thus?
I loved you ever : but it is no matter ;
Let Hercules himself do what he may,
The cat will mew and dog will have his day.   [*Exit.*
  King. I pray thee, good Horatio, wait upon him.
                                      [*Exit Horatio.*
 · [*To Laertes*] Strengthen your patience in our last
      night's speech ;
We'll put the matter to the present push.
This grave shall have a living monument :
An hour of quiet shortly shall we see ;
Till then, in patience our proceeding be.

SCENE II.   *Outside the castle.*

Enter HAMLET *and* HORATIO.

Hamlet.

BUT I am very sorry, good Horatio,
That to Laertes I forgot myself;
For, by the image of my cause, I see
The portraiture of his :
But, sure, the bravery of his grief did put me
Into a towering passion.

Hor.   Peace ! who comes here ?

Enter OSRIC.

Osr. Your lordship is right welcome back to Denmark.

Ham. I humbly thank you, sir.   Dost know this water-fly ?

Hor. No, my good lord.

Ham. Thy state is the more gracious ; for 'tis a vice to know him.

Osr. Sweet lord, if your lordship were at leisure, I should impart a thing to you from his majesty.

Ham. I will receive it, sir, with all diligence of spirit.   Put your bonnet to his right use; 'tis for the head.

Osr. I thank your lordship, it is very hot.

Ham. No, believe me, 'tis very cold; the wind is northerly.

Osr. It is indifferent cold, my lord, indeed.

Ham. But yet methinks it is very sultry and hot, or my complexion—

Osr. Exceedingly, my lord; it is very sultry, as 'twere,—I cannot tell how.   But, my lord, his majesty bade me signify to you that he has laid a great wager on your head : sir, this is the matter—

Ham. I beseech you, remember—

[*Hamlet moves him to put on his hat.*

Osr. Nay, good my lord ; for mine ease, in good faith. Sir, here is newly come to court Laertes ; believe me, an absolute gentleman, full of most excellent differences, of very soft society and great showing : indeed, to speak feelingly of him, he is the card or calendar of gentry, for you shall find in him the continent of what part a gentleman would see.

Ham. What imports the nomination of this gentleman ?

Osr. Of Laertes ?

Ham. Of him, sir.

Osr. You are not ignorant of what excellence Laertes is—

Ham. I dare not confess that, lest I should compare with him in excellence : but, to know a man well were to know himself.

Osr. I mean, sir, for his weapon.

Ham. What's his weapon ?

Osr. Rapier and dagger.

Ham. That's two of his weapons : but, well.

Osr. The king, sir, hath wagered with him six Barbary horses : against the which he has imponed, as I take it, six French rapiers and poniards, with their assigns, as girdle, hangers, and so : three of the carriages, in faith, are very dear to fancy, very responsive to the hilts, most delicate carriages, and of very liberal conceit.

Ham. What call you the carriages ?

Osr. The carriages, sir, are the hangers.

Ham. The phrase would be more germane to the matter, if we could carry a cannon by our sides.

Osr. The king, sir, hath laid, sir, that in a dozen passes between yourself and him, he shall not exceed you three hits : he hath laid on twelve for nine ; and it would come to immediate trial, if your lordship would vouchsafe the answer.

Ham. How if I answer "no ?"

Osr. I mean, my lord, the opposition of your person in trial.

Ham. Sir, if it please his majesty, it is the breathing time of day with me ; let the foils be brought, the
gentleman willing, and the king hold his purpose, I
will win for him an I can ; if not, I will gain nothing
but my shame and the odd hits.

Osr. Shall I redeliver you e'en so ?

Ham. To this effect, sir, after what flourish your
nature will.

Osr. I commend my duty to your lordship.

Ham. Yours, yours. [*Exit Osric.*] He does well to
commend himself, there are no tongues else for's turn.

Hor. You will lose this wager, my lord.

Ham. I do not think so : since he went into France,
I have been in continual practice ; I shall win at the
odds. But thou wouldst not think how ill all's here
about my heart : but it is no matter.

Hor. Nay, good my lord,—

Ham. It is but foolery ; but it is such a kind of
gain-giving, as would perhaps trouble a woman.

Hor. If your mind dislike any thing, obey it. I
will forestall their repair hither, and say you are not fit.

Ham. Not a whit ; we defy augury : there is special
providence in the fall of a sparrow. If it be now, 'tis
not to come ; if it be not to come, it will be now ; if it be
not now, yet it will come : the readiness is all. There's
a divinity that shape's our ends, rough-hew them how
we will.

[*Exeunt Hamlet and Horatio.*

SCENE III.   *A hall in the castle.*

KING, QUEEN, HAMLET, HORATIO, LAERTES, *and*
Lords, OSRIC, *and other* Attendants *with foils; a
table with flagons of wine on it. Flourish of trumpets.*

King.

OME, Hamlet, come, and take this hand from
me.

Ham. Give me your pardon, sir : I've done
you wrong ;

But pardon 't, as you are a gentleman.
Let my disclaiming from a purposed evil
Free me so far in your most generous thoughts,
That I have shot mine arrow o'er the house,
And hurt my brother.
   Laer.   I am satisfied in nature,
Whose motive, in this case, should stir me most
To my revenge.
I do receive your offered love like love,
And will not wrong it.
   Ham.   I embrace it freely,
And will this brother's wager frankly play.
Give us the foils.
   Laer.   Come, one for me.
   Ham. I'll be your foil, Laertes : in mine ignorance
Your skill shall, like a star i' the darkest night,
Stick fiery off indeed.
   Laer.   You mock me, sir.
   Ham. No, by this hand.
   King. Give them the foils, young Osric. Cousin
       Hamlet,
You know the wager ?
   Ham.   Very well, my lord;
Your grace hath laid the odds o' the weaker side.
   King. I do not fear it ; I have seen you both :
But since he is better'd, we have therefore odds.
   Laer. This is too heavy, let me see another.
   Ham. This likes me well. These foils have all a
       length?
   Osr. Ay, my good lord.
   King. Set me the stoups of wine upon that table.
If Hamlet give the first or second hit,
Or quit in answer of the third exchange,
Let all the battlements their ordnance fire ;
The king shall drink to Hamlet's better breath ;
And in the cup an union shall he throw,
Richer than that which four successive kings
In Denmark's crown have worn. Give me the cups ;
And let the kettle to the trumpet speak,

The trumpet to the cannoneer without,
The cannons to the heavens, the heaven to earth,
"Now the king drinks to Hamlet."
                    [*Flourish, and cannon shot off within.*
                              Come, begin :
And you, the judges, bear a wary eye.
  Ham. Come on, sir.
  Laer.   Come, my lord.   [*They play.*
  Ham.   One.
  Laer.   No.
  Ham.   Judgment.
  Osr. A hit, a very palpable hit.
  Laer.   Well; again.
  King. Stay; give me drink. Hamlet, this pearl is
    thine ;
Here's to thy health.
                    [*Flourish, and cannon shot off within.*
                              Give him the cup.
  Ham. I'll play this bout first; set it by awhile.
Come. [*They play*] Another hit; what say you ?
  Laer. A touch, a touch, I do confess.
  King. Our son shall win.
  Queen. The queen carouses to thy fortune, Hamlet.
  Ham. Good madam !
  King.   Gertrude, do not drink.
  Queen. I will, my lord ; I pray you, pardon me.
  King. [*Aside*] It is the poison'd cup : it is too late.
  Laer. [*Aside*] I'll hit him now.
And yet it is almost against my conscience.
  Ham. Come, for the third, Laertes : you but dally ;
I pray you pass with your best violence ;
I am afeard you make a wanton of me.
  Laer. Say you so ? come on.
    [*They play. Laertes wounds Hamlet ; they change
        rapiers, and Hamlet wounds Laertes.*
  King.   ·   Part them ; they are incensed.
  Ham. Nay, come, again.   [*The Queen falls.*
  ·*Osr.*   Look to the queen there, ho !
  Hor. How is it, my lord ?

Osr. How is 't, Laertes?

Laer. Why, as a woodcock to mine own springe,
 Osric;
I am justly kill'd with mine own treachery.

Ham. How does the queen?

King. She swounds to see them bleed.

Queen. No, no, the drink, the drink,—O my dear
 Hamlet,—
The drink, the drink! I am poison'd. [*Dies.*

Ham. O villany! Ho! let the door be lock'd:
Treachery! Seek it out.

Laer. It is here, Hamlet: Hamlet, thou art slain;
No medicine in the world can do thee good;
In thee there is not half an hour of life;
The treacherous instrument is in thy hand,
Unbated and envenom'd: the foul practice
Hath turn'd itself on me; lo, here I lie,
Never to rise again: thy mother's poison'd:
I can no more: the king, the king's to blame.

Ham. The point envenom'd too!
Then, venom, to thy work.

All. Treason! treason!

Ham. Here, thou incestuous, murderous, damned
 Dane,
Drink off this potion.—
Follow my mother. [*Stabs the King.*

Laer. He is justly served;
Exchange forgiveness with me, noble Hamlet:
Mine and my father's death come not upon thee,
Nor thine on me! [*Dies.*

Ham. Heaven make thee free of it! I follow thee.
I am dead, Horatio. Wretched queen, adieu!
You that look pale and tremble at this chance,
That are but mutes or audience to this act,
Had I but time—as this fell sergeant, death,
Is strict in his arrest—O, I could tell you—
But let it be. Horatio, I am dead;
Thou livest; report me and my cause aright
To the unsatisfied.

G

Hor.   Never believe it :
I am more an antique Roman than a Dane
Here's yet some liquor left.
 Ham.   As thou 'rt a man,
Give me the cup : let go ; by heaven, I'll have 't.
O God ! Horatio, what a wounded name,
Things standing thus unknown, shall live behind me !
If thou didst ever hold me in thy heart,
Absent thee from felicity awhile—
And in this harsh world draw thy breath in pain
To tell my story.
O, I die, Horatio ; .
The potent poison quite o'er-crows my spirit :
The rest is silence.   [*Dies.*

Curtain.

CHISWICK PRESS :—C. WHITTINGHAM AND CO., TOOKS COURT, CHANCERY LANE.